Praise for
The Audacity of Help
Obama's Economic Plan and the Remaking of America
By John F. Wasik

"No crystal ball—even President Obama's—can ever be perfect, but veteran business journalist John Wasik has experience in following economic intent through to economic reality. Wasik has taken the time to carefully sort out the impact of a stimulus program destined to be a significant page in history books."

—**Andrew Leckey,** Reynolds Business Journalism Chair, Walter Cronkite School, Arizona State University, and syndicated investment columnist for Tribune Media Services, Inc.

"Wasik has that rarest of abilities—to combine political philosophy with personal finance. He shows the Obama Administration and the taxpayer alike a path out of the economic fog. Wasik's critique without rage sheds light on a way forward for the administration."

—**Amity Shlaes,** Senior Columnist, Bloomberg News

THE AUDACITY
OF HELP

Also by
John F. Wasik

The Cul-de-Sac Syndrome:
Turning Around the Unsustainable American Dream

Also available from
Bloomberg Press

Making Sense of the Dollar:
Exposing Dangerous Myths about Trade and Foreign Exchange
by Marc Chandler

Collateral Damaged:
The Marketing of Consumer Debt to America
by Charles R. Geisst

Pension Dumping:
The Reasons, the Wreckage, the Stakes for Wall Street
by Fran Hawthorne

Aqua Shock:
The Water Crisis in America
by Susan J. Marks

A complete list of our titles is available at
www.bloomberg.com/books

Attention Corporations

This book is available for bulk purchase at special discount. Special editions or chapter reprints can also be customized to specifications. For information, please e-mail Bloomberg Press, **press@bloomberg.com**, Attention: Director of Special Markets, or phone 212-617-7966.

THE AUDACITY
OF HELP

Obama's Economic Plan and the Remaking of America

JOHN F. WASIK

BLOOMBERG PRESS
NEW YORK

This publication contains the author's opinions and is designed to provide accurate and authoritative information. It is sold with the understanding that the author, publisher, and Bloomberg L.P. are not engaged in rendering legal, accounting, investment-planning, or other professional advice. The reader should seek the services of a qualified professional for such advice; the author, publisher, and Bloomberg L.P. cannot be held responsible for any loss incurred as a result of specific investments or planning decisions made by the reader.

First edition published 2009

1 3 5 7 9 10 8 6 4 2

Library of Congress Cataloging-in-Publication Data

Wasik, John F.
    The audacity of help : Obama's economic plan and the remaking of America /
John F. Wasik. – 1st ed.
    p. cm.
    Includes bibliographical references and index.
    Summary: "The Audacity of Help explores how Barack Obama's campaign promises compare with the measures Congress has enacted, detailing what Obama has achieved and what is yet to be realized. The book evaluates how the stimulus package will affect health care, education, the environment, energy, taxes, and more, and includes analysis on which sectors will benefit most"–Provided by publisher.
    ISBN 978-1-57660-356-7 (pbk. : alk. paper)
    1. United States–Economic policy–2009 2. United States–Economic conditions–2009 I. Title.
HC106.84.W37 2009
330.973–dc22

2009025223

Mixed Sources
Product group from well-managed forests, controlled sources and recycled wood or fibre
www.fsc.org Cert no. SW-COC-002985
© 1996 Forest Stewardship Council

Planet Friendly Publishing
✔ Made in the United States
✔ Printed on Recycled Paper
Text: 100%   Cover: 10%
Learn more: www.greenedition.org

Printing on recycled paper helps minimize our consumption of trees, water, and fossil fuels.

The text of *The Audacity of Help* was printed on paper made with 100% post-consumer waste and the cover was printed on paper made with 10% post-consumer waste. According to Environmental Defense's Paper Calculator, by using this innovative paper instead of conventional papers, we achieved the following environmental benefits:

Trees Saved: 69 • Air Emissions Eliminated: 6,546 pounds
Water Saved: 31,527 gallons • Solid Waste Eliminated: 1,914 pounds

For more informatiom on our environmental practices, please visit us online at www.greenedition.org

To Kathleen Rose
Oui, nous pouvons!

CONTENTS

Preface

IN THE CITY'S FRONT YARD, set against the splendid Lake Michigan on a perfect, warm November day (a miracle in itself given Chicago's typically nasty weather from Halloween to Memorial Day), the hopeful gathered, attempting to get into a park that was tightly cordoned off to anyone without Secret Service clearance. It was November 4, 2008, and Barack Obama was about to make history.

"Who sent you?" was the first question barked at me by a security guard as I showed my press credentials at the gate of the media staging area. How ironic that this time-honored greeting of Chicago ward politicians would welcome my attempt to get a close look at Obama's election-day victory celebration. Alas, I did not obtain Secret Service clearance from the campaign in advance, so I was denied admission. I grimaced and muttered a mea culpa and walked around the perimeter of the park.

The energy was palpable approaching the campaign's epicenter. I closed my eyes and felt the dynamic pulse of optimism and pessimism competing for my attention. The potential dread of him losing because of some widespread fraud, which I am sure would have sparked mayhem, rang in my ears like a maddening tinnitus. Yet my auditory precognition reverberated with the prospect of him winning, an act that could restore some hope to the country and the world after eight destructive years. I chatted briefly with an African-American police sergeant. "It's been pretty quiet today—so far," he said, broadly smiling the whole time.

The fete was on hallowed ground in the history of the Republic. Abraham Lincoln was nominated in a long-forgotten place called the WigWam a mile north of the site, in an election that fomented the Civil War. An even more forgotten statue of Union General John Logan sat opposite the Obama fest site. Vendors were selling T-shirts with images of Martin Luther King and Obama. Some were emblazoned with "Rosa [Parks] sat so Martin [Luther King Jr.] could walk, so Obama could run, so our children could fly."

The Chicago police riots during the 1968 Democratic National Convention—when the cops beat up Vietnam War protesters—took place two blocks away. In the middle of that violence, Mayor Richard J. Daley blustered, "We are here to *preserve* disorder, not to create it." A few years earlier, Dr. Martin Luther King, marching in Marquette Park, was hit in the head with a brick a short bus ride from Obama's current home.

In the years since, much progress has come to the former "hog butcher to the world" and the nation. Jim Crow, apartheid in schools and public places, came and went in my lifetime. Voting rights came to minorities in the South. Americans landed on the moon several times. But despite that, a president, his brother, and Dr. King were assassinated, and Chicago remains one of the most segregated cities in the United States.

Who Is Obama?

Who is Barack Obama, the first person of color to be elected president? The son of a wayward Kenyan economist and a teenage mother. Community organizer. Harvard Law School graduate. University of Chicago Law School professor. State senator and U.S. senator. Once a little-known Illinois lawmaker, he ascended to his U.S. Senate seat when wealthy commodities trader Blair Hull bowed out of the race as details of his ugly divorce became public. His initial Republican opponent also had domestic issues.

With roots in the Midwest and Africa, Hawaii and Indonesia, Obama brings to the job a worldly genome and deep experience of many cultures. Because of his unique background, he may have a greater understanding of economic violence and social dislocation than any modern president.

When I met Obama during his Senate campaign in 2004, a voice echoed in my head: "This man *can* become president. He has the complete package." Millions agreed with me, taken by his calm confidence, intelligence, and eloquence. Unlike George W. Bush, he spoke to us, rather than *at* us. Obama organized a volunteer army of more than 13 million people, mostly through the Internet and text messaging. The Bush-weary twenty-first-century electorate was ready for Obama and was not put off by the strangeness of his name, his heritage, or his elite education.

During the campaign, he spoke to me and my neighbors in Prairie Crossing, about 45 miles northwest of Chicago and deep in Republican territory. At the time, and in many speeches thereafter, Obama echoed Lincoln when the sixteenth president spoke of his central idea of equality: "the principle that clears the path for all—gives hope to all—and, by consequence, enterprise, and industry."

By elucidating his concept of economic equality, Obama's message had a powerful resonance. Obama took office at a time when inflation was outpacing wage growth, companies were cutting pensions, and market disruptions and unemployment were leaving more than 45 million people without health insurance or retirement security. Obama also spoke to those raised to believe that they *would* be better off than their parents yet who were falling behind, losing their homes, and going bankrupt.

Big Troubles

With the economy a priority, the man who had been drawing millions of people to his speeches and ideas probably was not about to neglect the streets of Chicago or the forlorn urban pockets of despair from the Central Valley of California to the Bronx. Time will reveal if he is a man for all seasons; he first must assemble and execute an economic revival plan of historic proportions that may take years to transact, if it works at all.

His economic revival plans are ambitious and include everything from middle-class tax cuts to fixing the banking system. Everything that needed to be fixed was on the table in an effort to promote financial equality. Not all of it will survive congressional scalpels, but I hope to document what Obama promised and what Congress delivered.

The U.S. economy will be altered in some modest ways, but do not expect too much. Those who dismiss Obama as a socialist should look to his intellectual roots at the University of Chicago, the mother ship of market economics. The virtual Nobel Prize factory has cradled or crippled the global economy, depending on your worldview. Some of his top advisers are from that Hyde Park enclave, the spiritual home of free-market godfather Milton Friedman.

Will Obama be able to replace the more than 4 million manufacturing jobs that have been lost since 2000? Will he be able to repair and re-regulate the disemboweled financial system? Like any president, he may not have that much direct impact. It took World War II to fully re-engage the U.S. economy after a decade of FDR's New Deal programs.

And what of the human misery that is born of economic despair? The meanest streets of Chicago, where joblessness and street gangs claimed more than 400 lives in 2008, were just blocks away from Obama's celebration. Such an ongoing waste of human potential needs to end.

Obama's Insights

Fortunately, Obama is a uniquely qualified expert on economic violence. When he was a community organizer on the South Side of Chicago, he tried to restore a measure of dignity to tens of thousands of steel and other manufacturing workers who were impoverished by the brutal recession of the late 1970s and early 1980s.

It was ironic and utterly mean-spirited that he was ridiculed for his community efforts on the floor of the Republican National Convention in the summer of 2008. We could want for no greater authority on how neighborhoods and families could suffer during a recession than Obama.

I know of his work because I walked the same streets when I was writing (as a business-labor reporter for the long-defunct *Daily Calumet* newspaper) about the same people who had gone from decent wages and guaranteed benefits to poverty nearly overnight.

Their ranks were legion and included men such as Frank Lumpkin, a bare-fisted boxer who came from a Georgia sharecropping family to a decent job in a steel mill only to end up being a jobless coalition organizer when his mill (Wisconsin Steel) closed in 1980, depriving him and more than 4,000 others of back pay and benefits. Most of those same economic-security problems, sadly, were still hounding working Americans when I began this book. If you lost your job, you lost your health and retirement benefits—and a chance to get ahead. Why is this still a problem that bedevils our prosperity?

The Future

As I watched a gaggle of Chicago school kids march into Grant Park to see the spectacle of history on election day, my heart skipped a beat. As I was walking away from the park, they were strolling *into* it. The future was striding by. They were the heirs of everything Chicago had given the world: the modern electrical grid, commodities markets, transportation nexuses and countless tons of steel, machine tools, and candy. These children were players in the worldwide network, connected through aspirations and intelligence to street dealers in Rio, AIDS orphans in Tanzania, souk urchins in Cairo, and taxi drivers in Mumbai. Somehow, because of Obama's ascension to the highest office in the land, they had a feeling that they, too, could make a difference.

Would these future agents of change find room and hope in Obama's new network of progress, one so remarkable that it linked young and old, rich and poor in raising more than $600 million, a record amount for any campaign? Obama may not be able to boost incomes, restore sanity to financial markets, or even make health care affordable and available to all, yet he has provided a new agenda for tackling these problems. In his first days in office, he gave some direction by ordering the closing of the Guantanamo Bay prison, signing a law allowing women to sue for job discrimination, and lifting restrictions on stem-cell research.

As the ghosts of one of the most avaricious periods in American history continue to haunt our culture, will Obama restore market economics or simply create a new form of government-guided, compassionate social capitalism otherwise known as *Obamanomics*? Given the huge agenda he has taken on for reviving the economy and fixing the housing, financial, and mortgage markets as well as creating jobs, it will be this compelling fusion I call the "Green Deal." It will be holistic and looking far beyond his time in office. It is nothing less than restructuring the economy and industrial goals of the United States for the twenty-first century.

As a personal finance columnist for Bloomberg News, I have followed Obama's every move since he arrived on the national scene. Not only do I have a deep professional interest in seeing how he attempts to rebuild the economy, but also I want to know how individuals will benefit from his programs. I also want you to understand what he has promised and how Congress is reshaping—and sometimes sidelining—his ideas to deliver final pieces of legislation.

Genius for Reinvention

America has always possessed this genius for invention and reinvention. It's been a Valhalla for second chances. Illinois has had its share of makeovers and leaders who were pillars of power and purpose. Remember other renowned Illinois-bred politicians who reinvented themselves, including Ulysses S. Grant, who was transformed from merchant to general, and then got elected to two terms as president, eventually finishing his life as one of the greatest autobiographers in history; Adlai Stevenson, the intellectual turned presidential candidate and United Nations ambassador; and Ronald Reagan, the "B" actor turned governor, president, and Republican lion.

There was also the Great Emancipator, an icon whose prose Obama seeks to emulate. Lincoln himself was transformed from uneducated rail-splitter, failed shop owner, and railroad lawyer to win two short terms in the Illinois legislature and Congress and to become perhaps our most revered president. He was self-taught and born poor.

Whatever Obama will do, we can hope that he will not be the captive of the efficient and ruthless Chicago political machine or acquiesce to the powerful overlords of K Street and Wall Street. I trust he will stay true to Lincoln's dedication to the ideals of universal equality.

It is no small irony that Obama was inaugurated during the bicentennial of the births of both Lincoln and Charles Darwin. America is still on the tortured road to equality and evolves to seek the angels of our better nature. So goes the audacity of hope.

Thanks

I want to thank my fine editorial team at Bloomberg Press: Mary Ann McGuigan, Stephen Isaacs, and Yvette Romero; my agent, Robert Shepard; and my ever-patient wife, Kathleen, and daughters Sarah and Julia.

THE AUDACITY
OF HELP

The Ownership Society doesn't even try to spread the risks and rewards of the new economy among all Americans. Instead, it magnifies the uneven risks and rewards of today's winner-take-all economy. . . . That's not a recipe for sustained economic growth or the maintenance of a strong American middle class. . . . Fortunately there's an alternative approach, one that recasts FDR's social compact to meet the needs of a new century.

—Barack Obama, *The Audacity of Hope*

A Brief History of Obamanomics

Hope floated Barack Obama into the presidency. Elected with the boreal tailwind of an electorate facing a deep recession, buffeted by the myriad failures of the previous administration, and an old-fashioned lack of confidence in the status quo, the candidate for change had Herculean tasks ahead of him. The economic underpinnings of the American Dream were popping like rivets in a submarine that had gone too deep in the ocean. The most visible malady was the economy: in 2008, the stock market suffered its worst loss since 1937. Global credit markets nearly shut down, threatening a devastating depression. Millions of homeowners were either in or facing foreclosure. Average household income wasn't beating inflation.

"Something has gone terribly wrong with the American dream," wrote Kathleen Parker in the *Washington Post* the week before Obama's inauguration. "No longer is a college degree—or even an advanced degree—a guarantee of employment or job security."

Few Americans felt like they were getting ahead anymore, and more than 10 million were pounding the pavement. It was this vexing economic insecurity that propelled Obama's "change" and "Yes, We Can" campaign to the White House.

Why did the American people entrust an unknown, not-quite one-term senator from Chicago with the highest office in the land—one who promised just a broad outline of a plan for revival? Imbued with soaring intelligence, a gift for language, and jazz-age cool, Obama deftly delivered a disciplined message: I will create jobs, expand health care, improve environmental protection, and rebuild the country's sagging energy infrastructure. In many ways, his Green Deal was closer to Harold Ickes's (Franklin D. Roosevelt's Interior Secretary) utopian vision for the New Deal reforms FDR ramrodded through Congress during his first 100 days. Obama, too, aimed for the political stratosphere, knowing that Americans yearned for effective leaders, even in the depths of their despair. Alluding to Lincoln, FDR, John F. and Robert Kennedy, and Martin Luther King Jr., Obama's speeches not only told Americans what he hoped to accomplish but also articulated his blueprint for remaking America.

Obama took on the most immediate financial crisis and vowed to tackle looming unfunded liabilities that threatened to further wreck the retirements of baby boomers and their children. Just three days before his inauguration, he pledged a new "bargain" for Medicare and Social Security—that is, trying to find a way to sustain both of the huge, popular programs.

As if that wasn't enough to add to his impossibly gargantuan agenda, Obama also promised to create a new financial regulatory system that would better police the complex global markets that were still staring into the abyss as he took office. Pragmatism met the age of reckoning.

Was he still in campaign mode in his first 100 days, unnaturally confident, or not fully aware of the hydra he was about to face? Estimates of what it would take to attack the immediate economic maladies had risen to $1.2 trillion on the eve of his assumption of power. That was in addition to the $12 trillion pledged or lent to various institutions and companies by early 2009. Perhaps the intoxicating adulation that permeated the country before and during his inauguration had altered his sense of reality? Cleaning up the economic mess was one crisis. Making health care affordable and efficient was another. Social Security and Medicare were still the third rails of American politics. On top of all that, he called for the creation of 3 million to 4 million jobs. History would judge whether he would be seen as a twenty-first-century FDR—or a P. T. Barnum.

New Deal Reborn?

It was convenient to draw parallels between the New Deal and Obama's Green Deal. Both programs were geared to create jobs quickly, get the economy moving again, and attempt to instill some public confidence in the role of government. George W. Bush had become the baby boomers' Herbert Hoover, for the most part naively trusting market forces to repair the vast damage of an unregulated, greed-obsessed financial services juggernaut. FDR, of course, had it much worse when he took office in March 1933. One-quarter of the workforce was jobless. More than 26,000 businesses and 10,000 banks failed, eventually prompting "bank holidays" to give the government time to think and attempt to stem the losses. In the immediate aftermath of the 1929 crash, there was no financial regulation to speak of, so the greed that had ruled most of the 1920s turned back on itself to destroy the rest of the economy. Unlike today, the Federal Reserve Board and Treasury Department were feeble players during the 1930s.

While scholars continue to debate the lasting impact of the New Deal on the economy, it's indisputable that Roosevelt put millions of people back to work on projects that continue to provide social benefits. The most successful of Roosevelt's "alphabet soup" programs was the Civil Works Administration. The agency put 4 million citizens to work by the end of 1934. Thousands of public works projects were tackled, including roads, bridges, schools, parks, playgrounds, hospitals, airports, flood-control facilities, and privies.

Another make-work agency was the Civilian Conservation Corps, which employed as many as 3 million "soil soldiers" who built 97,000 miles of truck trails, 65,100 miles of telephone lines, and 3,470 fire towers and planted 1.3 *billion* trees. That last fact may have earned FDR the honor of being one of the great early champions against global warming (had he known it would later be a problem). Many New Deal programs, of course, didn't have much impact on the rest of the country, got mired in bureaucracy, or were political giveaways. The Public Works Administration, for example, bestowed most of its funding on New York City, thanks to the influence of its scrappy mayor, Fiorello La Guardia, and his powerful parks commissioner, Robert Moses, notes historian T. H. Watkins.

As with Obama's vision, New Dealers were accused of attempting to create a socialist utopia. "Utopian goals?" said Ickes in 1934, when posed a question about the real intent of the New Deal. "Yes, utopian indeed, but I do not apologize for suggesting that Utopia is a proper goal for us to strive for and that we are worthy of such a realm if we can achieve it."

What Went Wrong

Like FDR, Obama proposed a lofty agenda that will concentrate on creating employment and eventually economic security for working Americans. As a president who has a deep sense of history—it's evident in his speeches, writing, and policy proposals—Obama stated in his *Audacity of Hope* that "today, the social compact that FDR helped construct is beginning to crumble." Obama was distressed that job, retirement, and health security had been dismantled because the painful excesses of free-market policies wouldn't protect the country in a global economy. European, Japanese, and Canadian workers don't have to worry about their pensions or health care. In a global marketplace, Americans simply can't compete with countries that have a better social safety net.

"If the guiding philosophy behind the traditional system of social insurance could be described as 'We're all in it together,'" he continues in *Audacity*, "the philosophy behind the Ownership Society seems to be 'You're on your own.'"

What had been sold as a panacea during the 1990s and the first decade of the twenty-first century, the market economy, blew up with the triple explosions of the dot-com, housing, and credit bubbles. Wall Street and bankers sold the myth that stocks and homes were guaranteed ways to wealth. Over the past thirty years, they convinced employers to dump hundreds of thousands of guaranteed, defined-benefit retirement plans for 401(k)-like plans, which subjected employees to unchecked market risk.

Homeowners wanting to participate in the American Dream by building home equity succumbed to the promise that adjustable-rate . mortgages—which actually subjected them to the perils of credit markets—would create solid nest eggs. Entrepreneurs and, increasingly, corporate employees were hawked the idea of fending for themselves for health insurance, where they were effectively punished in the form . of unaffordable rates for any preexisting conditions. Such was the big lie of the ownership society. It was the obverse of the New Deal philosophy. It was a *raw* deal.

Coupled with the myth that ordinary consumers could somehow make rational, informed decisions in an unpoliced market economy was the Nero-like fallacy during the Bush years that nothing was wrong with our energy infrastructure or climate. The surge in oil (to $147 a barrel) and gasoline ($4-plus per gallon) prices in the middle of 2008 showed how utterly senseless this policy had been. The popularity of former Vice President Al Gore's *An Inconvenient Truth*, which won him both an Academy Award (for the movie version of his book) and a Nobel Prize for Peace, illuminated the folly of the Bush regime's anti-environment policies. Hurricanes, cyclones, and precipitation cycles have become more intense. Drought and forest and wildfires ravage densely populated regions, causing famine, dislocation, and war.

The Bush administration's criminal inattention to the victims of Hurricane Katrina in 2005 was emblematic of his disconnect from human reality (New Orleans is still a shell of its former self). It was pathological neglect like this that spurred much of the Obama Green Deal. Obama links a need for a new social compact with employment, education, and environmental concerns.

If most of his programs survive the contentious legislative process, Obama will have succeeded in reviving social capitalism, a blend of humanistic service, pragmatic government supervision, and some free-market principles. Better yet, if his initiatives excel in launching private-sector investments—and broad-based employment from inner cities to Silicon Valley—in clean energy, infrastructure, broadband expansion, and exportable technologies, he may even be seen as a social or *compassionate* capitalist.

The Green Deal is the spiritual heir of the New Deal, only much more focused on creating an economy specifically rebuilt for the twenty-first century. After all, FDR never believed capitalism was *dead*, he only sought to build new institutions and preserve old ones that failed because of an overreliance on unfettered market forces. Although a stern critic of market forces, Obama is attempting to frame humanistic economics in a different light: government can work to create a stronger private sector while creating jobs, educating everyone, rebuilding our infrastructure, addressing climate change, and helping the poor.

Basic Obamanomics

Boiled down, what Obama promises is a more *ecological* sense of shared responsibility. By ecological, I'm referring to interrelationships within society and the economy and not just the environment. Green jobs for inner-city residents mean better education and opportunity. Reshaping the energy infrastructure translates into less dependence on foreign energy sources, lower greenhouse gas emissions, and lower home-ownership expenses. Can the more than $350 billion the U.S. spends annually on energy imports be rechanneled into domestic energy production and jobs? Obamanomics provides the impetus to transform the United States into a greener economy.

This *new* economy, in Obama's plan, means redefining connections between government investments and economic growth. Spending money on health-record digitization, renewable energy, and general education will better position the United States to compete in global trade. More affordable and portable health care will create more economic security for everyone, particularly entrepreneurs.

Job creation and economic stimulation, naturally, topped the "to-do" list—in addition to a comprehensive bank bailout. The $787 stimulus plan passed by Congress, the focus of most of this book, was the first salvo. In his January 8, 2009, speech, when he introduced the main parts of his "American Recovery and Reinvestment Plan" (which I refer to throughout simply as the "stimulus" plan), he echoed FDR and laid the groundwork for his economic policy on the ruins of the ownership society and the botched bailouts of 2008:

> If nothing is done, this recession could linger for years. The unemployment rate could reach double digits. Our economy could fall $1 trillion short of its full capacity, which translates into more than $12,000 in lost income for a family of four. We could lose a generation of potential and promise, as more young Americans are forced to forgo dreams of college or the chance to train for the jobs of the future. . . . This crisis did not happen solely by some accident of history or normal turn of the business cycle, and we won't get out of it by simply waiting for a better day to come, or relying on the worn-out dogmas of the past. We arrived at this point due to an era of profound irresponsibility

that stretched from corporate boardrooms to the halls of power in Washington, DC. . . . Banks made loans without concern for whether borrowers could repay them, and some borrowers took advantage of cheap credit to take on debt they couldn't afford. Politicians spent taxpayer money without wisdom or discipline, and too often focused on scoring political points instead of the problems they were sent here to solve. The result has been a devastating loss of trust and confidence in our economy, our financial markets, and our government.

A Brief History of the Bush-Era Bust

Returning to recent history, it's essential to know how the economic crisis evolved to comprehend where Obamanomics might lead the country. The "Age of Froth" (based on an epic Alan Greenspan understatement when asked by Congress about his view of the housing market in 2006) is over. The days of cheap credit, rampant home appreciation, stock market gains, and easy living ended with several bangs and whimpers. The aftershocks were felt and heard by Obama during his eighteen-month campaign. This boiled-down narrative will bring you up to speed.

2006

The Age of Froth Ends. The U.S. housing market peaked with a significant number of homes financed by subprime, Alt-A adjustable loans for the credit-challenged.

2007

The Thrill Is Gone. The burst housing bubble started to release demons like Pandora's box. Housing prices started to decline nationwide, led by areas that experienced the highest appreciation. Home sales crawled to a virtual stop, and builders started to fold. Subprime lenders failed while major banks felt the pain of their overexposure to toxic mortgage securities. Falling home prices forced a downward spiral of home values in neighborhoods in which foreclosures were most pronounced. Homeowners in Arizona, California, Florida, Michigan,

Nevada, and Ohio were stung hardest because credit-challenged homeowners in adjustable-rate mortgages faced rate resets that made their monthly payments unaffordable. They were trapped because they couldn't refinance or sell their homes.

MARCH 16, 2008

Bye, Bye Bear. Hounded by a run and its heavy exposure to mortgage-related debt and securities, the investment banking firm Bear Stearns was forcibly merged by regulators into JPMorgan Chase for $10 a share (the initial price was $1 a share).

JULY 11

Big Failures, Big Bailout. When credit and stock markets nearly collapsed from the housing crisis, Congress decided to pass the first of several bailout measures. Although a huge mortgage and housing bill was signed by President George W. Bush in late July, the legislation did almost nothing to halt the spiral of 8,500 American homes a day slipping into foreclosure. Overall, it was projected that one in eight U.S. homeowners would suffer this fate over the next five years unless further action was taken. There was no end in sight for the housing crisis in mid-2008. As the International Monetary Fund stated, "a bottom for the housing market is not visible." Like many aggressive lenders in the bubble, California savings and loan IndyMac was seized by regulators, making it one of the largest thrift failures in history.

Foreclosure filings more than doubled in the second quarter over the previous year because millions of homeowners were falling behind and couldn't handle higher payments on adjustable loans. The measures in the first bailout were feeble:

- ♦ First-home buyers were given a refundable tax credit of as much as $8,000 "to help reduce the existing stock of unoccupied homes." This was little or no help to those who were struggling with payments or foreclosure. It was (then) actually an interest-free loan that had to be paid back, so it was a paltry incentive.

♦ Refinancing into Federal Housing Administration–guaranteed fixed-rate loans was available if distressed borrowers qualified (few did). Borrowers, however, had to share their equity gains—if any—with the government. Only owner-occupied homes without additional loans qualified.

♦ Some $4 billion in grants for "assistance" was earmarked for "communities hardest hit by foreclosures and delinquencies."

To further bolster the secondary mortgage market, the first bailout propped up mortgage enterprises Federal National Mortgage Association (Fannie Mae) and Federal Home Loan Mortgage Corporation (Freddie Mac), the two largest mortgage lenders and guarantors. They were taken over by the government and placed in conservatorship. That meant they were effectively seized by the Treasury, which also gained broad authority to buy their stock and bonds. A new, tougher watchdog agency was to police their recovery. Originally chartered to insure and buy mortgages, the two companies had nearly all of their common stock wiped out as their stock prices were measured in pennies. Together, they held $5.2 trillion in housing debt—half of the U.S. mortgage market.

SEPTEMBER 7 TO 17

Mortgage Madness. Three days after Freddie and Fannie were seized, Lehman Brothers put itself on the auction block after reporting $4 billion in mostly mortgage security losses. Treasury Secretary Henry Paulson and Federal Reserve Chairman Ben S. Bernanke chose *not* to extend a lifeline, forcing the bank to file for bankruptcy. Deemed too small to be rescued, it became the largest business bankruptcy in U.S. history and triggered even more panic selling in all stocks.

Meanwhile, Merrill Lynch, once the nation's largest brokerage, felt the heat from short sellers (those who bid down a stock price in hopes of making a profit) and rushed into the arms of Bank of America in a hasty acquisition. Yet another player in mortgage securities, American International Group, Inc., the world's largest insurer, found itself in a bind and besieged by short selling because of its derivative positions on toxic mortgage derivatives. This time, though, regulators transacted an

$85 billion loan and partial buyout. Sensing that short selling was a bit of a problem, the Securities and Exchange Commission temporarily banned some forms of the practice.

SEPTEMBER 18

Deep Credit Freeze. A global panic ensued as banks nearly halted short-term lending. The resulting liquidity crisis forced central banks from the United States, Europe, and Asia to pump $180 billion into credit markets. Bernanke and Paulson pleaded with Congress to pass an emergency plan to save the financial system. Paulson's original proposal was three pages long and granted him extraordinary powers. The Treasury guaranteed money market fund assets to stop a run on these short-term debt vehicles. The financial system was on the brink of collapse.

OCTOBER

Congress to the Rescue. After Senator John McCain briefly suspended his campaign and returned to Washington to appear to negotiate the bailout package, Congress balked at Paulson's original plan. Stock markets around the world crashed again, forcing Congress to compromise on a $700 billion measure that proposed to buy bad debt from banks and stop foreclosures. Little money from the Troubled Asset Relief Program (TARP) reached struggling homeowners as foreclosures continued at a record pace through the end of the year. Grilled by a congressional panel on his failed role as a regulator during the bubble, Alan Greenspan told lawmakers that the crisis "has turned out to be much broader than anything I could have imagined. It has morphed from one gripped by liquidity restraints to one in which fears of insolvency are now paramount." He coyly called the debacle the collapse of a "whole intellectual edifice."

NOVEMBER

Yes, We Can. On the heels of the worst financial crisis since the Great Depression, Barack Obama was elected forty-fourth president of the United States, capturing about 53 percent of the vote. Democrats added to their majorities in the House and Senate yet didn't get the sixty votes needed to override filibusters in the Senate. Ushered into office during the worst economic situation since the 1930s, the Democrats campaigned on economic salvation. Congressman Barney Frank (D-Massachusetts), chairman of the House Financial Services Committee and one of the authors of TARP, said he was peeved that there was almost no accountability for the bailout spending. Banks were receiving the money, but very few were lending. Foreclosures continued unabated as banks restricted credit. Meanwhile, bank executives and brokers continued to pay bonuses and dividends.

DECEMBER

Jobs Evaporate. The U.S. Labor Department reported that more than a half million jobs were lost in November as the economy appeared to be in a free fall. For the year, the job loss was the worst since 1945. Another half million–plus would be jobless by the end of the month. The National Bureau of Economic Research, the arbiter of the nation's economic health, reported that the country had been in a recession for a year. The Standard & Poor's 500 Index, a gauge of the largest stocks in America, was down 38 percent for 2008, the largest single decline since 1937. Retirement and college funds invested mostly in stocks were ravaged. All told, some $8.5 trillion was either lent or committed to saving the financial system. That was more than half of the U.S. gross domestic product at the time. After receiving $148 billion in government assistance designed to spur lending, the thirteen biggest U.S. banks *reduced* their loan volume between the third and fourth quarters of 2008. They mostly continued their lobbying and generous executive-compensation practices unabated. Gross domestic product plummeted 6.2 percent in the fourth quarter, signaling the worst economic downturn since 1982.

JANUARY 2009

Reality Show Time. As Obama's inauguration approached, his economic team feverishly negotiated with congressional leaders to craft an economic stimulus plan. Because of the stock-market decline and dropping of short-term bond yields to nearly zero, state pension funds reported losses of more than $800 billion. States from California to Rhode Island asked for federal assistance. Corporate pension plans reported that they were underfunded by $409 billion, erasing the surplus of $60 billion they had at the end of 2007.

On January 13, Bernanke stated that the government might need to buy or guarantee bad bank assets if the economy was to recover. "Fiscal actions are unlikely to promote a lasting recovery."

President-elect Obama told President Bush he would order the Treasury to "limit executive compensation and dividend payments" from banks receiving TARP funds (most bank executives avoided pay and dividend cuts while accepting taxpayer money). Obama's economic team outlined its own bailout objectives, which include reforming financial regulation, curbing foreclosures, getting credit flowing again, and maximizing "the role of private capital and [planning] for exit of government intervention."

Facing criticism from congressional leaders that his proposed $775 billion economic plan wasn't aggressive enough, Obama considered increasing tax credits for alternative energy while paring small-business job-hiring incentives, which might prove difficult to monitor. The president-elect proposed creating nearly 4 million jobs in energy, infrastructure, health care, and education as well as providing state relief and income-tax rebates. In its revised version of the Obama revitalization plan, the U.S. House drafted an $825 billion package and added temporary health-care subsidies, a patch for the hated Alternative Minimum Tax, college tuition credits, and numerous incentives for alternative-energy and energy-efficiency measures.

Bank of America, the largest remaining bank by assets, said it desperately needed a $138 billion government loan to stay afloat. The bank had digested money losers Merrill Lynch and Countrywide Financial during the height of the 2008 meltdown. Both companies carried billions of subprime mortgages and securities on their books.

Moving Forward

The bust has cost the world economy some $30 trillion. Obama's team needed to defibrillate the sorry state of the American financial, housing, and labor markets and find a way to get consumers spending again. The deleveraging of America was prompting an age of reckoning. U.S. household debt was 173 percent of gross domestic product when Obama took office. People were borrowing more than they were earning. Net worth was down 11 percent in 2008.

The rapacious financial-services industry succeeded beyond its wildest dreams, plunging everyone from Main Street to the most sophisticated Wall Street firms into unsustainable debt. At the height of the debt bubble, the financial sector accounted for 40 percent of all corporate profits, up from 10 percent in the early '80s. As Obama scrambled to put his stimulus plan in place, estimates for further bank bailouts were exceeding $2 trillion.

New York University Professor Nouriel Roubini, who predicted the credit crisis, claimed, "Most of the U.S. banking system is insolvent. You will eventually have to nationalize U.S. banks."

Is it realistic to expect that Obamanomics will somehow tame or slay the triple-headed beast of the financial market collapse, consumer insecurity, and a global recession? Would it be insane to expect that in reviving a badly damaged economy he could create a phoenix of a greener, smarter, and efficient "new" economy and transact his Green Deal? It's a political thriller that is unfolding as you read this and will be a testament to his team's flexibility, creativity, and mettle—if they achieve at least one of these goals. Should his administration come up short, then the electorate will not be forgiving if jobs continue to evaporate and credit tightens. The success of the plan will depend on how effective his stimulus plan is within the next two years. Much of the infrastructure spending, though, will not be helpful in the short term and will take several years for its economic impact to be realized.

In subsequent chapters, I will detail how each of Obama's new programs will have an impact on you personally, how you can benefit from them, and what investments you might consider for the future. As a way of showing you the political timeline, I present what the Obama team has promised (in their own words), what Congress delivered, and what it means for you now and in the future. I'll also look at unfinished business that Obama has said he hopes to address in the future.

We remain the most prosperous, powerful nation on Earth. Our workers are no less productive than when this crisis began. Our minds are no less inventive, our goods and services no less needed than they were last week or last month or last year. Our capacity remains undiminished. But our time of standing pat, of protecting narrow interests and putting off unpleasant decisions—that time has surely passed. Starting today, we must pick ourselves up, dust ourselves off, and begin again the work of remaking America.

—President Barack Obama, Inaugural Address, January 20, 2009

CHAPTER 1

First Aid and Income Boosters

B arack Hussein Obama took the oath of office as the forty-fourth president of the United States with his hand on Lincoln's bible (the same one used for the Great Emancipator's inauguration in 1861) and the promise that he would reconfigure the existing antihumanistic economic system with a new one based on unity, fairness, partnership, environmental progress, mindful policing, and sound finance.

Amid an inspiring, tearful, and history-making inauguration that drew more than 2 million spectators to Washington, Obama delivered a sober address that called for change and sacrifice. Wall Street, however, didn't get the message so clearly. Within days of the inauguration, news articles revealed that in early 2008, while Merrill Lynch was financially ailing, then-CEO John Thain spent more than $1 million redecorating his office. In December of the year, when Merrill was so distressed that Bank of America had to acquire it (Bank of America later found out Merrill suffered a $15 billion loss that quarter), Merrill directors approved approximately $4 billion in year-end bonuses to its brokers. Thain resigned after this was disclosed. President Obama called the bonuses "shameful," but ailing Wall Street firms still continued the practice. In March 2009, it was revealed that insurance giant American International Group, which had received $170 billion in taxpayer money to stay afloat, issued $165 million in year-end bonuses to its staff. The Age of Froth was not *quite* over for Wall Street elite.

From the New Deal to the Green Deal

Given the awful shape of the U.S. economy when Obama was inaugurated—gross domestic product shrank by an annualized rate of 6.2 percent in the fourth quarter of 2008—the most immediate thrust of Obamanomics was to create jobs and aid the unemployed.

But on a deeper level, Obama seeks to reinvigorate the American psyche and remake government's role in shaping the economy. His "Yes, We Can!" campaign slogan reverberated throughout America. A generation that was brought up to believe that in America you *could* get ahead was chastened, disheartened, and, in many cases, downright broke. Most households were losing badly to inflation as incomes leveled out in 2007 while retirement funds and the main nest egg—homes— were losing value in a debacle not seen since the 1930s. Obama was elected to fight the war of diminishing expectations, pitting Main Street against Wall Street, the destructive demons of the free market against the paternal vigilance of government.

Focusing on the restoration of prosperity, Obamanomics relies heavily on *humanistic* economics—that is, placing social concerns before the altar of economic expansion. Obama came into office knowing the economy would probably contract further, so he didn't make any pronouncements on growth of the gross national product. Instead of touting numbers, he emphasizes *people*-centered principles by focusing on health care and education. Having built much of his historic campaign with social capital—the powerful networks of people throughout the country, text messages, e-mail, and the Internet—Obama wants to show how social goals can be combined with capitalism. As he moves to remake the economy, his *social* capitalism is a stark rebuke of the folly of *laissez-faire* capitalism. Instead of a free-for-all in which only the well-positioned financial elite would benefit, he wants to create a culture of sharing and responsibility for the entire population.

Knowing that he had an FDR-like mandate in his first 100 days, Obama has seeded his revival of the American economy by focusing on energy, education, and health care. The nation's first African-American president went to work the day after he was elected. In his first few weeks in office, he issued a memorandum calling for higher vehicle fuel-economy standards, signed a legislation for children's health insurance, and banned certain kinds of employment discrimination. Nearly one-tenth of his stimulus plan—some $80 billion—provides funds for clean energy, high-speed rail, fuel-efficient vehicles, and weatherized public buildings. Throughout his campaign, which seemed to continue like a riveting ballad with endless refrains into the first two months of his term, he stressed the economic benefits of what he proposed. Clean-energy technology is not just an environmental mantra for lowering greenhouse-gas emissions; it means creating jobs and exports to China, Germany, and Japan. It translates into lower operating costs for industry and lower household utility bills. Government provides the seed money, and the private sector and populace reap the rewards.

Part of Obama's plan was designed to help people who need immediate aid: those who are unemployed, needing food and utility-bill assistance and struggling to pay their mortgages. The remainder of the stimulus was aimed at creating jobs and helping small businesses (see Chapters 2 and 3). Unlike the failed supply-side economic theories employed since the Reagan era, Obama puts a "bottom-up" theory to the test. He believes that by providing direct funding and tax credits to those rebuilding infrastructure and creating clean energy, he can restore jobs and tackle climate change and energy independence with one fell swoop.

Rather than providing tax cuts for upper-income Americans (those making more than $250,000 annually), Obama focused his breaks on middle- and lower-income groups. His assumption has been that providing relief and aid to the majority of Americans will make them more likely to create businesses and jobs. That's a short-term aid package that assumes that most of the help will be delivered through 2010 when most of the stimulus funding expires.

As a former University of Chicago Law School professor, he embraced many of the principles of market economics from the cradle of that philosophy, as do many people in his cabinet. Yet he sees greater value in dispensing with the pure, free-market orthodoxy and employing government as an agent of change. This isn't exactly the New Deal, and it's the polar opposite of Reaganism. In Obamanomics, government isn't the enemy; it can be a benefactor for shared social objectives, the middle class, and the poor. He cemented this vision in his first address to Congress on February 24:

> History reminds us that at every moment of economic upheaval and transformation, this nation has responded with bold action and big ideas. In the midst of civil war, we laid railroad tracks from one coast to another that spurred commerce and industry. From the turmoil of the Industrial Revolution came a system of public high schools that prepared our citizens for a new age. In the wake of war and depression, the GI Bill sent a generation to college and created the largest middle class in history. And a twilight struggle for freedom led to a nation of highways, an American on the moon, and an explosion of technology that still shapes our world. In each case, government didn't supplant private enterprise; it catalyzed private enterprise. It created the conditions for thousands of entrepreneurs and new businesses to adapt and to thrive.

Ultimately, the key to the success or failure of Obamanomics will be flexibility. Not all of his programs will have an immediate impact, and many will only be part of a multilayered solution to a problem. As with the New Deal era, he may have to employ several programs if the economy worsens. While confident, he doesn't initially appear to be unrealistic on his administration's ability to stem the economic decline, nor is he wedded to liberal or conservative orthodoxy on the best approach.

"You know, they are not expecting miracles," Obama said of what the American people expected of him on *60 Minutes* in late 2008. "If something doesn't work, they are going to try something else until they find something that does—although there are some parallels to the problems we're seeing now and what we saw back in the 1930s, no period is exactly the same—I think our basic principle is that this is a free-market system and that has worked for us, that it creates innovation and risk taking, I think that's a principle that we've got to hold onto as well. My interest is finding something that works."

Curing the Disease

How much will Obama truly emulate the radical New Deal reforms? In creating work, regulating markets, and remaking government policy to accommodate the forceful realities of a global economy, climate change, and the deleveraging of the financial sector, he needed to take bold actions. By the time the first leg of his recovery plan passed, some 3.6 million jobs had been lost the year before. If Obama is to remake the American economy, then he first has to get people back to work and heal the banking industry.

With his experienced, well-informed team of financial advisers, which included former Federal Reserve Chairman Paul Volcker, legendary investor Warren Buffett, and former Harvard president and economist Lawrence Summers, Obama had many briefings on the cause of the economic malaise well before he was elected. Based on how he spoke and presented himself during his campaign, debates, and interviews, he appeared to have a grasp of the dire shape of the economy. Most of the electorate bought the perception that he had a better approach to dealing with economic issues than his then presidential rival, Senator John McCain (R-Arizona).

The American financial pathology was fairly well studied before Obama took office. As Charles Kindleberger noted in his classic *Manias, Panics, and Crashes*, "Most economies are mostly healthy, but on occasion an economy can be infected with one or another economic virus." It may take years for Obama to alleviate the multiple maladies afflicting the U.S. economy, which have since stricken markets from Shanghai to Frankfurt. He might have to battle the economic pathogens one at a time with separate programs. Here's what he's up against.

Foreclosure Frenzy. The congressional bailout measures passed toward the end of 2008 and the stimulus package of early 2009 did almost nothing to stop foreclosures. Some $8.5 trillion was either lent or committed to saving the largest financial institutions while largely ignoring one of the root causes of the housing crisis: homeowners were overleveraged and priced out of their homes. When they obtained low-interest, adjustable-rate loans, all of these borrowers were completely exposed to credit-market risk. When interest rates rose, so did their monthly payments, largely making their mortgages unaffordable and triggering 3.2 million foreclosure filings in 2008, soaring 81 percent from 2007 and 225 percent from 2006, at the height of the bubble. Repossessions continued unabated in 2009, as up to 8 million people

faced foreclosure. Homeowners remained trapped in the downward
spiral because the resulting credit crunch made refinancing unavail-
able to most of them and sales were nearly impossible. The crash fed
on itself, and as more foreclosed homes came on the market at fire-
sale prices, values continued to drop. All told, by the time of Obama's
inauguration, home prices were down 20 percent from the market
peak on average and more than twice that in distressed areas such as
Arizona, California, Florida, and Nevada. If Obama wants to stem or
halt foreclosures, then his plan will need to be effective by doing the
following: (1) allowing people to stay in their homes either as renters
or under modified, more affordable terms; (2) making refinancing
possible; (3) buying the notes outright; or (4) finding a way to stabilize
the secondary mortgage market and put a floor under housing prices.
This one crisis is related to the others yet will be the most difficult
to solve.

Credit Conservatism. When banks are afraid that they won't get
repaid, they won't lend. They look for some sort of guarantees or
other assurances that they can make a profit. That's the essence of the
credit crunch, which spread like a virus after it became clear that all
of the mortgage securities and related derivatives had simultaneously
dropped in value, causing a market panic in mid-2007 that continued
through 2008 and into 2009. When lending shuts down, businesses
can't expand or operate normally, payrolls contract, jobs evaporate,
and few people can buy a house. The TARP (Troubled Asset Relief
Program or "truly anemic rescue plan")—which appeared to be
a boondoggle by the end of 2008—injected $350 billion (of the
$700 billion allocated) directly into banks and savings and loans. Yet
there was almost no accountability or congressional oversight on how
the money would be spent or curbs on executive compensation at the
time. Most of it did not appear to go into increased consumer or commercial lending.

Obama's team will have to find another way to boost the credit
markets long term without handing money directly to the banks.
Between the time he was elected and his inauguration, it became
painfully clear that his original economic manifesto would have a
higher price tag. The tab rose from about $600 billion originally

to $850 billion in late January 2009. Many economists called for a $1 trillion package.

Cleaning Up the System. Where were the watchdogs that were supposed to be policing the banking and brokerage industry in its packaging of bad mortgages? Who was watching the shadowy derivatives market, a series of bets on the quality of the debt being sold? The Securities and Exchange Commission, Commodity Futures Trading Commission, and Federal Reserve Board were utterly passive during the expansion of the bubble and the extreme leveraging used to fund it. More than $30 trillion was lost worldwide in the resulting bust. The New Deal approach is helpful, although markets are much more complicated and interrelated today. Modern regulation needs to be tailored to a global, modern economy. That will be a multiyear work in progress for Obama's team, one that won't happen overnight and will involve a thorough overhaul and reconstruction of existing agencies. As economist James Galbraith observed below in a Bloomberg News commentary from December 31, 2008, Obama's government needs to be a forceful leader on both stimulating the economy and restructuring regulation:

> The challenge facing the American government now comes in two parts. The first is to maintain spending in an economy that cannot, for the duration, draw spending power from the poisoned well of private finance. The second part must be to reconstruct the necessary economic functions of government—beginning with effective global financial regulation—for our own sake and as a model for the world.

Paying for It All. None of these fixes will be cheap. Unless offset by tax increases or budget cuts over time, several generations will be paying for them and may face soaring inflation as the government attempts to finance and pay off its more than $11 trillion national debt. While he transacts his bailout, Obama will need to cut waste from the federal budget in his "new bargain" as the deficit soars above $1 trillion. You can't leverage a country this way and not expect to pay the bill someday or face a lower standard of living. Social Security and Medicare also need to be funded for future generations. It's not realistic to expect the Chinese, Japanese, and Europeans to entirely fund this recovery through their purchases of U.S. Treasury securities. At some point, they will stop buying American IOUs. There's lots of pork to be trimmed from federal spending (see Chapter 10). Taxpayers are spending $100 billion to subsidize private insurers in the Medicare Advantage program. Billions are being wasted or sheltered from the Treasury in agricultural subsidies, offshore corporations, and countless tax breaks. More than $300 billion in taxes due aren't collected every year due to cutbacks in the Internal Revenue Service. Although Obama said he hoped to trim the federal budget deficit in four years, it remains to be seen if that will be possible if Congress continues to embrace wasteful earmark spending and lobbyists still have undue influence on legislators.

Congress will be the churlish gatekeeper on Obamanomics. All pieces of legislationing can be massaged, co-opted, and remade by K Street lobbyists and party leaders with some public input. What is unique about Obama's plan is that he used his cybernetwork of 13 million supporters (led by his campaign manager David Plouffe) to engage in the creation, lobbying, and sculpting of this legislation. This may mark the advent of a truly twenty-first-century legislative process, where average citizens, working through a large, coordinated network, are able to influence and direct the creation of laws.

Plan Details

To provide some perspective on the legislative process and how the severity of the economy morphed his original plan by the time of its passage, I first reviewed the original campaign literature ("what was promised"), then the final laws or policies enacted in the first 100 days of the Obama administration. At the end of each chapter is my analysis on how particular groups will benefit.

Even when the overall economy was growing, most American families were not sharing in this growth. The net worth of American families fell by more than $5 trillion in the fourth quarter of 2008, the largest drop in more than a half century of recordkeeping. As of January 2009, average weekly wages, adjusted for inflation, were lower than they were a decade earlier. Barack Obama and Joe Biden's overall economic plan will relieve the squeeze on families and foster bottom-up growth. But they are proposing that we implement several measures immediately.

TAX CUTS

What Was Promised: Obama proposed a permanent tax cut of $500 for workers and $1,000 for families. A first round of these tax credits would be mailed out by the IRS based on tax returns already filed for tax year 2007. In addition, Obama and Biden would extend these expedited tax credits to retired senior citizens as a down payment on his plan to eliminate taxes for all seniors making up to $50,000.

What Congress Passed: "Making Work Pay" Credit. Despite the politically savvy title, this is a limited credit that will pay a maximum of $400 to singles and $800 for those filing jointly. The credit gets reduced for those making more than $75,000 or $150,000 (filing jointly). It will apply retroactively to the beginning of 2009 for those who qualify (you need earned income) and will extend through 2010. You can either receive it as a reduction in payroll tax withholding or as a lump sum when you file your tax return. The credit offsets federal payroll taxes, giving you a modest raise for two years. Although Republican House members claimed that the credit would result in average savings of $1.35 per day, it has more value for lower-income workers, though probably not enough of an incentive to jump-start the economy or create many jobs. Those on fixed incomes or the disabled will receive a one-time payment of $250. It's estimated to help 95 percent of working families, according to congressional analysts.

EXTENDED UNEMPLOYMENT INSURANCE BENEFITS

What Was Promised: Millions of Americans are looking for work but are unable to find it in the weak economy. As of January 2009, more than one in five unemployed workers had been out of work for more than half a year—the highest level since early 2005. Obama supported extending unemployment insurance in the summer of 2008, but by mid-2008, 800,000 jobless workers exhausted those benefits and were

being left without any unemployment compensation. During the
campaign, Obama and Biden said Congress should immediately extend
unemployment insurance for an additional thirteen weeks to help the
families being hit hardest by the recession. In addition, they said, we
should temporarily suspend taxes on unemployment insurance benefits as a way of giving more relief to families.

What Congress Passed: Cobra Health-Care Subsidy. Under this
subsidy, if you are unemployed and are able to continue health
insurance from your employer (provided that they offered coverage
in the first place), the government will pay for 65 percent of your
premiums for up to nine months. It's only provided to those who were
laid off and made less than $125,000, or $250,000 for families.

♦ **Unemployment insurance exemption.** In addition, if you're
out of work and collecting unemployment pay, $2,400 of the
benefits will not be subject to federal income tax. (However, a
more substantial break would have been to exclude all *jobless*
benefits from taxes so that people out of work are not taxed.)
Benefits were extended to twenty weeks in most states and to
thirty-three weeks in states with the worst unemployment rates
such as Michigan, California, and Rhode Island. The average
payment was also raised by $25 per week.

PENALTY-FREE HARDSHIP WITHDRAWALS
FROM IRAs AND 401(k)s

What Was Promised: Many families are going to be facing unique
economic hardship throughout 2009. To help these families pay
their bills and their mortgages and make it through these tough
times, Obama called for legislation that would allow withdrawals
of 15 percent, up to $10,000, from retirement accounts without
penalty (although subject to the normal taxes). This would apply
to withdrawals in 2008 (including retroactively) and 2009.

What Congress Passed: Congress did not allow penalty-free
withdrawals.

WITHDRAWALS FROM 401(k)s AND IRAs FOR SENIORS

What Was Promised: In 2008, those over age 70½ were required to start withdrawing funds from their individual retirement accounts. Obama called for the Treasury to temporarily suspend the required withdrawals for retirees over that age 70½. This will give seniors the flexibility they deserve—to forgo withdrawals if they choose or to take those withdrawals tax free if they need those resources to pay their bills.

What Congress Passed: Although not part of the stimulus package, Congress passed a provision in December 2008 that waived required minimum distributions from individual retirement accounts, profit-sharing money-purchase plans, and certain 457 retirement plans through 2009. That means retirees can keep money in these funds for an additional year without being forced to make withdrawals.

FUNDS TO COUNTERACT HIGH HEATING COSTS

What Was Promised: Obama promised to supplement the existing funding through the Low Income Home Energy Assistance Program (LIHEAP) to ensure that cold-weather states could cushion the impact of high energy prices for their residents in the winter. The Energy Information Administration said that consumers would pay a projected $1,137 to heat their homes from October 1, 2008, to March 31, 2009—15 percent more than the previous year's heating outlay—and homeowners who use heating oil rather than natural gas could see increases of 23 percent compared to the previous year. As part of his $25 billion state fiscal relief package, Obama's plan promised to supplement existing LIHEAP funding to help state programs expand coverage to more residents while continuing to provide a meaningful benefit.

What Congress Passed: Home Energy Credits. Congress offers a maximum credit of 30 percent for several energy-efficient improvements (as defined by the IRS). It applies to any installations made after December 31, 2008, and before January 1, 2011.

Improvements that qualify include insulation, skylights, exterior windows, water heaters (all types), boilers, heat pumps, exterior doors, wood stoves, central air conditioning, advanced "main air circulating fans," and certain metal roofs. This is a great incentive for those who need to replace a water heater, furnace, or air-conditioning system. Old limits applied to solar energy units ($2,000), geothermal ($2,000), and wind ($500) for each kilowatt of capacity are repealed in the new law. The only exception is a $500 cap on fuel-cell property and several other items. That's a boon for anyone interested in spending tens of thousands of dollars for alternative-energy systems. LIHEAP received no additional funds.

ADDITIONAL TAX INCENTIVES PASSED

Child Tax Credit Limit Lowered. The Child Tax Credit, aimed to help impoverished families, provides a federal income tax credit of up to $1,000 for every child under age 17. The income minimum to qualify for the refundable credit was 15 percent of the taxpayer's earned income in excess of $8,500 in 2008. For 2009 and 2010, the minimum is $3,000.

Expanded Earned Income Tax Credit (EITC). The IRS defines the EITC as a tax break for low- to moderate-income working individuals and families. The stimulus package temporarily increased the tax credit for families with three or more children. The old threshold applied to families with two or more children and a credit equal to 40 percent of the family's first $12,570 of earned income. Under the recovery act, the threshold would be 45 percent of that amount and cover families with three or more children. The phase-out range for married couples filing jointly would be raised by $1,880 to $21,420. The expansion is only good through 2009 and 2010. Some employers can pay the credit in advance through payroll. You have to make a request because it won't happen automatically.

Alternative Minimum Tax (AMT) Exemptions Raised. Congress raised the amount of income exempt from the dreaded AMT to $46,700 for singles and $70,950 for those filing jointly. Although helping those in high-tax coastal states (mostly in California, New Jersey, and New York), it will do almost nothing to create jobs—unless you're a tax preparer or accountant. Some 26 million families will be helped through 2009.

Sales Tax Write-Off on Vehicles. You'll be able to deduct state, local, and excise taxes on cars, light trucks, recreational vehicles, and motorcycles through 2009. The break is only given to those who earn less than $125,000 or $250,000 for joint filers.

Who Benefits Most?

The unemployed are the most immediate beneficiaries of the new legislation passed by Congress. Extension of food stamp, health, and unemployment benefits is the first aid in this kind of crisis. Immediate income tax relief will be less effective. Estimates are that workers may not see extra money in their paychecks until mid-2009, when most employees will see a reduction in their payroll taxes.

Gaining modest help from extending corporate health benefits— provided they were covered by an employer to begin with—the unemployed get a break if they face losing their health-care coverage. But those remaining jobless for long periods will not benefit at all. Most laid-off workers are likely to lose their health-care benefits immediately. If they are eligible to continue medical coverage under the Cobra law, they typically pay the entire group premium, which averages more than $1,000. Because monthly jobless benefits range from $800 to $1,600 (depending on the state), millions more will become uninsured.

Largely thrown in to gain Republican support, the individual tax cuts are least likely to stimulate the economy. In times of distress, small amounts of government dollars are likely to be spent on paying off debts. Those who fear job losses will not be going out to buy big automobiles. Both progressives and conservatives are critical on the ability of tax credits to boost an economy. "Tax credits are often bad policy," writes Robert Kuttner in *Obama's Challenge.* "They blow huge holes in the tax code. . . . They turn the IRS into a social policy agency, a job for which it is ill suited."

Conservative economist Martin Feldstein also doubts the potency of tax givebacks. "Experience shows that lump-sum tax cuts are largely saved or used to pay down debt. Only about 15 percent of last year's (2008) tax rebates led to additional spending."

The infrastructure funds will boost a wide range of employers (see Chapter 2), although this money will take much longer to flow into the economy. An estimate by the Congressional Budget Office in late January 2009 projected that three quarters of the big-project spending would be pumped into the economy by early 2011.

Much of the plan was designed to help state and local governments stem the loss of tax revenue while creating or saving jobs. School districts would receive more than $40 billion to help balance budgets, avoid staff cutbacks, and modernize schools. Almost $90 billion went to aid states in paying Medicaid bills.

What Needs to Be Done

The bulk of the first portion of the Obama stimulus plan provides immediate aid and tax breaks. Nearly $300 billion—more than one-quarter of the package—is for tax breaks or direct aid such as extending unemployment insurance. Although this won't create any jobs, it is the triage component of the plan that will ease the pain.

The Biggest Beneficiaries in the Stimulus Plan

- **Those in dire financial need.** More than $300 billion is targeted for the unemployed and state governments for Medicaid funding and education programs.
- **Public works.** More than $160 billion will be spent on roads, water systems, bridges, broadband access, high-speed rail, alternative energy, and other infrastructure projects.
- **Middle- and low-income households.** About $116 billion was set aside for payroll-tax cuts.

When President George W. Bush took office, the jobless rate was 4 percent, with more than 6 million people out of work. By the end of his second term, unemployment nearly doubled to about 7 percent with more than 10 million people pounding the streets. The fractured ideology that tax cuts would compel those in the highest brackets to start businesses and create jobs has never been proven and has been a sorry myth ever since the Reagan administration. Yet conservative Republicans cling to that fairy tale, hoping to obstruct Obama's progressive agenda.

House leader John Boehner and his counterparts were initially charmed by meeting Obama amid the first wave of stimulus legislation, but they walked away chanting the same incantation: more tax cuts, more tax cuts. Individual tax-rate reductions, though, are rarely effective in reviving the economy in a meaningful way. In mid-2001, some 92 million Americans received about $38 billion in rebates. What did they do with the money? Only 22 percent told researchers Matthew Shapiro and Joel Slemrod of the National Bureau of Economic Research that they would spend it. The majority either paid down debt or saved the money. Few jobs were created. The Bush administration and Congress approved tax reductions in 2001, 2003, 2004, and 2006—that's nearly $2 *trillion* through 2010, yet employment continued to plummet through 2008.

Robert Borosage, codirector of the Campaign for America's Future, one of the key progressive groups seeding Obama's initial agenda, decried the conservatives' barnacle-like attitude on supply-side incentives, which George H. W. Bush once called "voodoo economics." "Conservatives have learned nothing from the collapse of their economic policies and the decline of their political fortunes," Borosage stated in January 2009. "By staying in obstructionist mode they are placing themselves on the wrong side of history."

There was little in the stimulus legislation that would address the long-term cost structure of the programs receiving the emergency funding. Wracked by loss of in-state revenue, forty-two states and the District of Columbia were facing $51 billion in budget shortfalls in 2009 and a projected $94 billion in shortfalls in 2010. A prolonged recession or continued housing downturn would make things worse and may necessitate a second stimulus measure. At best, the first package attempts to keep a supertanker-sized problem from sinking further.

Of the package, $136 billion was to be channeled to the states for bolstering Medicaid, school staffing, and public-safety services; the states needed hefty support to keep essential programs such as Medicaid running. Because Medicaid programs are jointly funded by federal and state governments, they will continue to drain state coffers unless cost controls or systemwide reforms are put in place. The larger issue is the inefficiency of running more than five different public health programs: Medicaid (for the poor), Medicare (for the elderly and disabled), veterans' funds, and separate funds for federal and state governments. That's in addition to another program for children and private employers. Future health-care overhauls should consider consolidating some or all of these systems into one entity. A single-payer system could reap some huge economies of scale (see Chapter 8).

More Tax Changes in the 2010 Budget

The administration's proposed 2010 budget offers more assistance to middle-class and poor families while reining in tax breaks for the wealthy. Here are some highlights of how Obamanomics plans to pay for some of its programs and modestly address income inequality:

- ◆ The Making Work Pay Credit would become permanent. The paltry $400 rebate for individuals and $800 for joint filers would stay in the tax code, fulfilling Obama's pledge to cut taxes for "95 percent of taxpayers."

- ◆ The earned income tax and saver's credits would be expanded for low-income families.

- ◆ Enrollment in 401(k) plans would be mandatory. Workers would be automatically enrolled in the outdated company savings plans, although they could opt out.

- ◆ Deductions would be trimmed for those making more than $200,000 a year ($250,000 for families). Most itemized deductions would be capped at 28 percent, while the top two rates would be bumped up to Clinton-era levels of 36 percent and

39.6 percent (the highest rate) in 2011. These changes could generate up to $1 trillion in revenue, which Obama said he would channel into health care.

♦ The 15 percent preferred rate on capital gains and dividends would be raised to 20 percent, easing the disparity between wage and investment income. Yet you will still be taxed at the highest possible "ordinary" income rates on pensions, savings interest, and salaries.

♦ Farmers making more than $500,000 annually would see their agricultural subsidies taken away.

Falling Short

Obama's policies fall short in addressing a crying need to streamline and rework America's 10,000-page tax code. The initial stimulus package will not simplify taxes or skew tax incentives toward saving and away from speculation. None of the tax breaks for buying or owning real estate were pared; in fact, they were sweetened (see Chapter 7).

The meager payroll tax break doesn't address the fact that wages were taxed at higher rates than capital gains or dividends. Under the Bush-era tax policies, workers fared worse than investors and will continue to do so unless the code is revised. Obama's team, should it be interested in tax reform, will need to examine this issue closely not only for future sources of revenue but also to restore parity between those who buy and invest in securities and real estate and people with modest or limited portfolios.

Obama also needs a comprehensive, flexible, and long-range plan to address homeownership issues. In 2008, homeowners lost more than $3 trillion from home equity, approximately $6 trillion total since the market peaked in 2006. A workable plan would have to include either fully nationalizing seized mortgage insurers Federal Home Loan Mortgage Corporation. and Federal National Mortgage Association (Freddie Mac and Fannie Mae), or providing mortgages near the cost of Federal Reserve funds (less than 1 percent as of January 2009) and extensive mortgage counseling and oversight (see Chapter 7).

Yes, we will put people to work repairing crumbling roads, bridges, and schools by eliminating the backlog of well-planned, worthy and needed infrastructure projects. But we will also do more to retrofit America for a global economy. That means updating the way we get our electricity by starting to build a new smart grid that will save us money, protect our power sources from blackout or attack, and deliver clean, alternative forms of energy to every corner of our nation. It means expanding broadband lines across America so that a small business in a rural town can connect and compete with their counterparts anywhere in the world. And it means investing in the science, research, and technology that will lead to new medical breakthroughs, new discoveries, and entire new industries.

—President Barack Obama, January 8, 2009

CHAPTER 2

Rebuilding Infrastructure, Creating Jobs

In January 2009, following data saying the economy contracted in the last three months of 2008, Obama stated, "The recession is deepening, and the urgency of our economic crisis is growing." With the economy in shambles, Obama pushed hard for the stimulus package, which he saw as necessary for turning around the ailing economy. But even though congressional Democrats widely supported the stimulus package, selling the plan to Republicans was tough.

Obama openly courted a bipartisan strategy when he took his stimulus plan to Congress. He lobbied GOP members on Capitol Hill and hosted a rare cocktail party for them in the White House. Calling the economy a "continuing disaster" for families, he created a task force for the middle class and put Vice President "you don't mess with Joe" Biden in charge of it. He also signed executive orders bolstering unions and beefing up vehicle-mileage standards. He appeared to have momentum going into tough negotiations with leaders in the House of Representatives. Speaker Nancy Pelosi had a broad majority behind her, so she easily rubber-stamped most of Obama's initiatives. But Republicans did not agree to the plan so readily.

Though Republicans were okay with pouring billions of dollars a month into rebuilding Afghanistan and Iraq, when Obama approached them with his stimulus package, they suddenly became fiscal conservatives again; they bemoaned the addition to the national debt and argued there would be little in the spending package to create jobs.

Ultimately, the House passed the $819 billion stimulus package in January 2009 in a 224–118 vote—and without a single Republican supporting it.

With the House victory on his stimulus bill in hand in January 2009, there was little margin for error in the fractious Senate, where Obama initially said his legislation would win with eighty votes. But then a GOP backlash spread like a virus from the House to the upper chamber; Obama could likely count on only fifty-eight Democrats and independents to vote on his plan, but he needed sixty votes to avoid a bill-stopping filibuster.

The Senate debated the stimulus for the first week of February 2009 and nearly ended up deadlocked. Most conservative GOP senators became born-again converts to the fiscal austerity religion. While Obama campaign manager David Plouffe urged online Obamaites to organize economic recovery "house meetings" during that week to mobilize support for the president's plan, the Congressional Budget Office bolstered the Republicans by estimating that most of the stimulus's impact would reach the economy in 2010. With the deficit now estimated to exceed $1.4 trillion (in 2010), Senator John McCain (Obama's former presidential rival) dug in his bloc for lengthy debates against the initial package before the Senate. Having vacuumed the House momentum out of the legislative process, the conservatives invoked their hatred of the spending program in harsh tones.

"This is the largest generational *theft* bill in the history of mankind," said Senator Tom Coburn (R-Oklahoma) on the Senate floor February 6, 2009. "We will lose $90 billion through running the funds through inefficient bureaucracies." Senator Lindsey Graham (R-South Carolina) estimated that creating four million jobs would cost taxpayers $212,000 per job.

By the end of that contentious week, Rahm Emanuel, Obama's chief of staff, had brokered a deal to bring Republican moderate senators Susan Collins and Olympia Snowe (both of Maine) and Arlen Specter (Pennsylvania) on board to give the plan just enough votes to pass the Senate. (Arlen Specter subsequently changed parties altogether and became a Democrat in April 2009.) The Senate passed a revised $787 billion package in February 2009 in a 60–38 vote; the cost of the moderate compromise was $140 billion in cuts. Under the brokered deal, states and schools would receive less emergency aid, and clean-energy firms received fewer subsidies. Obamanomics was crippled but not dismembered. The question remained how the plan would create new jobs, especially those from small businesses, which generate the majority of new positions.

Job Creation

You do not need to go far to notice that America's skeleton has major osteoporosis. New York's water tunnels are leaking millions of gallons of precious water. Los Angeles can never seem to get enough water. Chicago's ancient elevated-rail system (the "el") is rusting away. Just miles from the White House, suburban Maryland's 5,500-mile system of water pipes sprang a few leaks, among the more than 4,000 over the past two years. (Just a few days before Obama's inauguration, the state reported 252 leaks.)

As soon as the proposal passed, every member of Congress, governor, and mayor was waiting to spend checks from the $787 billion package: approximately $130 billion targeted for infrastructure projects and $20 billion for renewable energy. There could not have been a more savvy way of kicking off the first 100 days of the most anticipated presidency in a generation.

Yet will these projects amount to the usual sops of political patronage? Will the party bosses be licking their chops and calling in their chits for years to come? Much of the success—and perceived fairness—of the infrastructure spending program will depend on how worthy the projects are that ultimately receive funds. Will there be swimming pools for wealthy neighborhoods? Bridges to nowhere? Only a responsible and active auditing team that is relatively untainted by pernicious lobbying efforts will be able to ensure the money goes where it is truly needed.

In an economic emergency, the name of the game is putting people back to work and getting them to spend money and pay taxes. The U.S. Conference of Mayors listed more than 18,000 "shovel-ready" projects in 800 cities that it hoped would accomplish

just that. The city of Los Angeles alone detailed 325 items that
were expected to create more than 80,000 jobs. Wherever the
money goes, it will barely touch the existing need for infrastructure repairs because there are countless projects that have been on
officials' wish lists for years. The mayors' list valued projects worth
more than $139 billion. The bulk of the city requests—15,000
projects—were for roads, streets, water systems, and community
block grants. Ultimately, most of these projects will not be funded,
so the stimulus plan is like a start-up fund for a much larger infrastructure agenda. The list's price tag had grown from that of the
conference's original wish list on December 19, 2008, which cited
$96 billion worth of projects.

Education and Infrastructure

What Was Promised: Obama promised to save 1 million jobs through
immediate investments for roads, bridges, and schools. The emergency plan would make $25 billion immediately available in a jobs and
growth fund to help ensure that in-progress and fast-tracked infrastructure projects are not sidelined and to ensure that schools can

The Long-Term Wish List: "Shovel-Ready" Infrastructure Funding

- $32 billion for a "smart" utility grid
- $30 billion for highways and bridges
- $30 billion to modernize public buildings
- $10 billion for community block grants, green jobs, and school modernization
- $10 billion for mass transit (buses, trains, and stations)
- $10 billion for science research facilities
- $6 billion for improved internet access in rural areas
- $6 billion to replace aging sewer lines
- $4.2 billion for communities to purchase and reoccupy vacant foreclosed homes
- $4 billion for more police officers and equipment
- $3.1 billion for public land improvements
- $3 billion to expand congested airports
- $1.15 billion for "better land and seaports"

meet their energy costs and undertake key repairs starting in the fall of 2009. The plan, which also calls for modernizing the nation's water systems, would be the largest increase in our nation's mass-transit system since the creation of the national highway system in the 1950s. This increased investment is necessary to stem growing budget pressures on infrastructure projects. In an environment where we faced elevated unemployment levels well into 2009, making an aggressive investment in urgent, high-priority infrastructure served as a triple win by generating jobs to boost our economy in the near term, enhancing U.S. competitiveness in the longer term, and improving the environment by adopting energy-efficient school and infrastructure repairs.

What Congress Passed: Infrastructure Funding. Congress approved $98 billion in funding for infrastructure projects, substantially surpassing Obama's original request of $25 billion. The funding includes the following:

- ◆ $39 billion for electrical-system improvements, with the money going toward modernizing and creating a "smart" grid, broadband installation, advancing battery technology, and awarding energy-department grants (see Chapter 4);

- ◆ $29 billion for public works, including everything from street repairs to bridge reconstruction;

- ◆ $18 billion for cleaning up toxic waste, upgrading municipal water systems, and flood prevention;

- ◆ $8.4 billion for public transit to help repair and upgrade public-transportation systems;

- ◆ $8 billion for high-speed rail to reduce reliance on air travel (this is in addition to the $8.4 billion for public transit improvements).

PORT SECURITY AND IMPROVING VETERANS' HOUSING

What Was Promised: Obama promised to enhance the security of ninety major ports. He also promised to aid troops and veterans by making much-needed repairs to military-housing units and accelerating the modernization of Veterans Administration medical facilities.

What Congress Passed: Increased Funding. Approximately $4 billion was targeted for improving military facilities in the stimulus plan, and more was promised in the budget. Nearly $3 billion was set aside for homeland security programs.

AUTO INDUSTRY

What Was Promised: Obama originally pushed for $50 billion in loan guarantees to help the auto industry retool, develop new battery technologies, and produce the next generation of fuel-efficient cars here in the United States.

What Congress Passed: Funding for Auto Industry. Congress tabbed $2 billion for advanced vehicle batteries and will buy 17,600 new, American-made fuel-efficient vehicles for the General Services Administration. The least politically popular of all bailout measures—though not related to the stimulus package—was the $110 billion lent to Chrysler and General Motors by early June 2009.

ADDITIONAL MEASURES PASSED

In addition to the measure above, Congress also approved more than $8.5 billion for biomedical research. Doled out by the National Institutes of Health, this block is intended to help find cures for Alzheimer's disease, heart disease, Parkinson's disease, and cancer.

Who Benefits Most?

Building infrastructure will be the most visible way of creating jobs. Every road, bridge, water, and sewer project will carry signs telling taxpayers where the money is coming from, and news reports will contain thousands of examples of how the money will be spent.

Some 35,000 jobs also could be created for every $1 billion spent on transportation infrastructure. This helps asphalt pavers, laborers, welders, and nearly every construction-trade worker. The $7 billion set aside for broadband installation throughout the rural United States, part of the plan's science and technology/electrical infrastructure allocation, would mostly benefit telecommunications companies and the people installing these systems.

Municipalities receiving grants for street, road, or water-system improvements will be able to put those dollars to work immediately on projects that have been planned (and delayed) for years. Areas with veteran's hospitals and military camps will also see an increase in construction-trade jobs. Funds were earmarked for the Army, Air Force, Marines, Navy, and reserve units.

On the energy front, companies ranging from local utilities to specialized energy auditors would suddenly find their expertise and services in demand. Because the federal government is one of the largest users of electricity on the planet, it would help every taxpayer to lower government-utility bills; however, do not look for a tax rebate based on an estimated $2 billion in savings anytime soon.

Also, it would be unlikely that any company benefiting from the infrastructure spending boom will show any dramatic increases in stock price as you read this. The general recession has hurt nearly every corporation in some way. Long-term investments are best in these areas because it may take years for companies to realize any profits from these projects. In addition, the market long ago anticipated whatever short-term gains these firms will achieve, so forget about a quick killing.

Specific companies that will benefit (stock ticker symbols are in parentheses) include those in the following table.

My general caution on all Obamanomics-related investments applies here: you can roll the dice on individual companies, sectors, and funds, but your best bet is a broadly diversified portfolio. Also, do not assume that only American companies will benefit; many of the leaders in energy systems and infrastructure development are based overseas, so a global mutual or exchange-traded fund will give you the best exposure to them. In that spirit, I recommend the iShares S&P Global Infrastructure Index Fund (IGF), which owns a broad base of companies ranging from TransCanada Corporation (TRP), a pipeline and power company, to Macquarie Infrastructure (MIG), which owns bridges, toll roads, and tunnels throughout North America. An even more diversified portfolio

Company	Product or Service
ADC Telecom (ADCT)	Network systems
3M Co. (MMM)	Solar, water
Akeena Solar Inc. (AKNS)	Solar systems
Bombardier Inc. (BBD/B)	Railcars
Caterpillar Inc. (CAT)	Earth-moving equipment
Cemex SAB (CX)	Cement
Cisco Systems Inc. (CSCO)	Network systems
Chicago Bridge & Iron (CBI)	Steel construction
Dell Inc. (DELL)	Computers
Danaher Corp. (DHR)	Power lighting
Emcor Group Inc. (EME)	Electronic systems
Emerson Electric (EMR)	Engineering, construction
Fluor Corp. (FLR)	Energy construction
Foster-Wheeler Ltd. (FWLT)	Construction
Hochteif AG (HOT GY)	Construction
Lindsay Corp. (LNN)	Irrigation
Lockheed Martin Corp. (LMT)	Information systems
Manitowoc Co. (MTW)	Crane manufacturing
McDermott International Inc. (MDR)	Energy services
Olympic Steel (ZEUS)	Steel distributor
Owens Corning Inc. (OC)	Insulation materials
Qwest Inc. (Q)	Broadband, telecom
Skanska AB (SKAB SS)	Building
Terex Corp. (TEX)	Trucks, cranes
Trinity Industries Inc. (TRN)	Construction, railcars

Source: Bloomberg News, Bloomberg L.P.

comes in the Vanguard Total (VT) World Stock Index exchange-traded fund.

What Needs to Be Done

The ecology of spending on public projects will shape the future of how we live. Few people can argue that repairs to water and sewer systems are not essential if we are to function as a civilized society. And in the interests of public safety, crumbling bridges and roads need to be fixed immediately. But should America be building new highways and adding to the sprawl that directly fueled the housing crisis?

The way the major project money is allocated will also determine how Obama's policies *could* reshape the United States. If his administration focuses on giving the lion's share of the funds to cities and suburbs, then it could trigger a new focus on urban renewal. A dollop of money spent on the most neglected states in the union, from Mississippi to Appalachia, might signal a subtle war on poverty. After all, all politics are local, and all politicians love to brag about what they "brought home."

There probably will not be much chance that expensive mega-projects, such as citywide light-rail systems or a large-scale upgrade of Amtrak, will receive a green light (there wasn't enough money in the initial stimulus). Although the price tags of many of the biggest projects will look large, their average scale will not be because so much money has to go to so many places.

Rural areas that may be struggling to attract jobs and keep families in agriculture may continue to suffer population losses—unless the broadband initiative is fully funded and implemented over the next four years ($7 billion might not be enough to complete high-speed Internet systems throughout rural America—see above). Will ex-urban regions receive their share of funds for large projects such as prisons and military bases? That's not certain, although it's certainly not anywhere near the top of the Obama team's priority list. What about megacities that are crying out for large-scale public transportation improvements and expansion? Again, those funds will not be fully available as part of the initial stimulus package. It will not be anywhere near recent stimulus spending in China, where a new subway system has opened every year from 2002 through 2008. (In contrast, the United States has opened forty-five new prisons in that time.)

If the Obama administration uses the stimulus spending as a template for future, long-term infrastructure policy, then it would mark a radical shift if the bulk of the public works dollars are redirected away from road building. According to the Congressional Budget Office (CBO), the largest single category for capital spending for decades has been highways. In 2007, the United States spent $32 billion (in 2006 dollars) on roads. That is more than twice the amount spent on mass transit, water resources, and aviation systems *combined.* The CBO estimates that $41 billion spent on mass transit and aviation is "economically justifiable"—that is, this spending will provide private and social benefits that at least equal economic costs; these dollars do the most good for the greatest number of taxpayers.

Larger projects that received some seed funding through the initial stimulus package loom. California, Florida, the Midwest, the Northeastern states, and Texas have sought high-speed rail. It makes sense as a way to link large metropolitan areas that are hundreds of miles apart and often inefficiently served by airlines. Yet Obama's first stimulus package provided what amounts to research and engineering money for these large, needed public works projects. A California high-speed line that would link Los Angeles to San Francisco is estimated to cost $45 billion; California voters only approved $10 billion in borrowing in November 2008. Other huge projects include modernizing the nation's air-traffic-control system ($20 billion or more); tunnels in Miami, New York, and Seattle ($14 billion); building New York's Second Avenue subway; a Dulles Airport train into downtown Washington, DC ($5 billion); and various other plans to build bridges, modernize ports, and relieve rail congestion.

STIMULUS NOT ENOUGH

The Obama plan originally set aside approximately $120 billion for infrastructure and science projects such as upgrading the utility grid, highways, bridges, and water systems and rehabbing public

President Obama announced an acceleration of the stimulus program on June 8 to create an estimated 600,000 jobs in the second 100 days of the Recovery Act. In the first 100 days, the administration claimed it created 150,000 jobs and made funds available for 4,000 transportation projects, many of which are displaying the administration's omnipresent stimulus plan logo. While it's always difficult to verify job creation, these projects will be high-visibility and designed to show the stimulus funds at work. This announcement doesn't represent new funding; it was designed to expedite job creation and create more publicity for the stimulus projects. At the time of the initiative, the administration was under criticism for not creating more jobs as the unemployment rate hovered above 9 percent and officials warned it may go higher. To track the distribution of stimulus funds, check www. recovery.gov or www.propublica.org.

The acceleration is intended to do the following:

- **Enable 1,129 health centers in fifty states and eight territories to expand service to approximately 300,000 patients.** This Health and Human Services program will create jobs and support efforts to improve access to quality, comprehensive, and affordable care.

- **Begin work on projects at ninety-eight airports and more than 1,500 highway locations.** Projects will include runway construction at selected airports to increase capacity, and interstate repaving projects to reduce congestion.

- **Fund 135,000 education jobs.** The Recovery Act funds will help offset losses in local and state revenues by keeping education workers on payrolls.

- **Make improvements at ninety veterans' medical centers across thirty-eight states.** Veterans Administration Medical Centers will be targeted for rehabilitation.

- **Hire or retain approximately 5,000 law enforcement officers.** These funds will be used to hire new officers while forestalling cuts that would be due to lower local tax revenues.

- **Start 200 new waste and water systems in rural America.** These projects will replace outdated water mains and build wastewater treatment facilities for small communities.

- **Fund projects in 107 national parks.** Largely starved of funding during the G.W. Bush Administration, the National Park System will receive funds for shelved projects.

- **Support cleanup work at twenty Superfund sites.** Superfund sites (toxic waste dumps) on the National Priority List will gain funding for clean-ups.

- **Create 125,000 summer youth jobs.** Work will be provided for summer programs.

- **Initiate 2,300 projects at 359 military facilities.** Department of Defense projects focus on outdated living quarters and "greening" military facilities throughout the country.

Source: http://www.whitehouse.gov/recovery/roadmap/

buildings, according to the Congressional Research Service. Yet the total need is estimated to be more than $1.6 *trillion*, according to the American Society of Civil Engineers, which published a report card on infrastructure conditions a few weeks after Obama took office.

What does the $1.6 trillion price tag cover? Let's start with a plane ride. Before you even take your seat, billions have been spent on control towers, runways, lights, radar systems, and airport facilities. Because more people are flying than ever before in a global economy, the system is in need of constant repair and upgrading. The air-traffic-control system, for example, has needed a major modernization for decades. Record delays are endemic in nearly every major airport because of infrastructure inadequacies. The Federal Aviation Administration estimates that at least $40 billion is needed for the civil aviation system just to keep up with the estimated 1 billion passengers who will be flying annually within the next ten years.

Get queasy at the thought of turbulence? Driving a vehicle is expensive as well. Get behind the wheel of your car and traverse the many potholes and traffic jams in your area. Crumbling or inadequate roads cost American motorists some $67 billion a year, or $710 per motorist—and that is just to fix the highways and bridges. We collectively lose the equivalent of 4.2 billion hours just sitting in traffic, costing the economy about $78 billion a year in terms of lost working hours (not to mention lost family time).

Are you a smarter commuter who takes public transit? Federal spending on the public-transportation systems lags the amount needed by some $6 billion annually. That makes highway repair numbers loom even larger because nearly half of all Americans do not have access to public transportation.

Of course, infrastructure involves much more than driving and flying. Here's a short list of some other pressing funding needs as noted by the civil engineers:

Brownfield Reclamation. Places where former landowners have left toxic waste can be reclaimed for future use, but taxpayers have to pay to clean them up. There are about 24,000 of these sites in 188 cities, covering more than 96,000 acres. Redeveloping these waste sites has resulted in more than $400 million in annual revenue since 2003.

Dams and Levees. Approximately $100 billion is needed to maintain these water-retention structures. More than 4,000 "unsafe or deficient dams" and 150 levees are in danger of breaking.

Water Systems. Some $400 billion is needed to maintain drinking and wastewater systems.

Inland Waterways. By the year 2020, almost 80 percent of the 257 locks in the country's 12,000-mile system will be "functionally obsolete." The cost to repair or replace the locks is $125 billion.

Public Parks and Recreation. These facilities face a $7 billion maintenance backlog. They are beneficial to the economy, supporting

More Infrastructure Spending in Budget

The Obama administration spread even more funding requests for infrastructure in its 2010 budget. Here are some of the major proposals:

- set up a national infrastructure bank that would receive $5 billion annually for general public works projects;
- allocate $5 billion for high-speed rail projects between 2010 and 2015 in addition to the $8 billion already allocated in the stimulus plan;
- give the U.S. Environmental Protection Agency nearly $4 billion for clean-water and drinking-water funds for more than 2,000 projects (if passed, the budget increase will be the largest in the agency's history);
- give rural areas $1.3 billion through the U.S. Department of Agriculture for broadband expansion;
- allocate $1 billion to the Department of Housing and Urban Development for an affordable-housing trust fund;
- give clean energy technologies a massive $40 billion boost in the form of loan guarantees for alternative energy (wind, solar), greenhouse gas reduction, carbon dioxide storage, and air pollution projects;
- give the nation's antiquated air-traffic-control system $800 million; and
- allocate funds to the Department of the Interior, which was starved under the Bush administration, including $100 million for the National Park Service and $50 million to promote renewable energy.

more than 6 million jobs and contributing more than $700 million annually to the U.S. economy.

Schools. The National Education Association estimates it would take $322 billion to physically repair public schools.

Railroads. Both freight and passenger railroads are bottlenecked in the current system, which needs more than $200 billion through 2035 to handle growth in traffic. Because freight trains are three times more fuel efficient than trucks, they can figure prominently in reducing the nation's total energy expenses.

PAYING FOR THE BIG BUDGET

One glaring subject that Obama avoided in the campaign and early days of his presidency was how to pay for infrastructure over time and how it will dovetail with an overall strategy to address climate change. Conservative Democrats and Republicans generally object not only to increasing the federal deficit but also to tax hikes. Unless huge cuts are made to other large budget items, which is unlikely during a recession, the Treasury will need to sell more debt to pay for the new spending, most likely to the Chinese, Japanese, and Europeans. At a certain point, investors in our debt may decide that the paltry after-inflation returns don't equal the political benefits of buying the notes. No one knows when that day will come, but it *will* happen; when it does, it could shut down the debt-financing juggernaut that is keeping the world's largest economy afloat.

There may be no way of getting around the fact that gasoline taxes (or carbon-based levies on fuel, vehicles, or buildings) need to be added or raised. The 18.4-cent levy on gasoline and 24.3-cent surtax on diesel fuel have been unchanged since 1993. Those taxes brought in $39 billion in 2007. The CBO projects an economically justifiable investment of $132 billion annually to keep highways in good repair. Filling this funding gap will have to involve some sacrifice and extra dollars from those who use the roadways. Each year, $44 billion could be created by boosting the fuel tax by 25 cents a gallon.

Recovery.gov: Keeping Tabs on How Your Money Is Spent

Want to track how the stimulus plan funds are being distributed? The White House set up a Web site—www.recovery.gov—to help you see where the money goes. It's part of the administration's move toward transparency.

This is what the administration hopes this tool will do:

- As the centerpiece of the president's commitment to transparency and accountability, recovery.gov will feature information on how the act is working, tools to help you hold the government accountable, and up-to-date data on the expenditure of funds.
- The first incarnation of recovery.gov features projections for how, when, and where the funds will be spent, including the proportions that different states and sectors of the economy are due to receive. As money starts to flow, far more data will become available.
- The site will include information about federal grant awards and contracts as well as formula grant allocations.
- Federal agencies will provide data on how they are using the money. Eventually, prime recipients of federal funding will provide information on how they are using their federal funds.
- The site will use interactive graphics to illustrate where the money is going, as well as estimates of how many jobs are being created, and where they are located. There will also be a search capability to make it easier for you to track the funds.

Keeping infrastructure functional and updated over time takes trillions of dollars. It will be fascinating to see how—and if—the Obama administration tackles this funding goliath after the need for immediate stimulus has passed. A national infrastructure bank or trust fund, as proposed in the 2010 budget, could become a permanent institution overseen by trustees who are independent of Congress. This entity, if managed prudently and free of political earmarking, might be able to avoid the pork-barrel process of awarding federal dollars to the well-heeled few. Until then, the first wave of federal dollars may be a short-term boost, but will not address the long-term aging of the nation's backbone.

Encouraging new industry means giving more support to entrepreneurs. . . . We will work, at every juncture, to remove bureaucratic barriers for small and start-up businesses—for example, by making the patent process more efficient and reliable. And we will help with technical support to do everything we can to make sure the next Google or Microsoft is started here in America.

—Barack Obama, June 16, 2008, Flint, Michigan

CHAPTER 3

Bottom-Up Economics:
Small-Business Benefits

As Congress passed the stimulus package, it seemed like one of the economy's most consistent job generators—small businesses—were initially left behind. Obama's idealistic campaign rhetoric regarding small businesses disappeared as his team prepared a comprehensive package that would deal with the rapidly deteriorating employment crisis in early 2009. There was no nod to small employers in his inaugural speech either. Strapped by the credit crisis and recession, countless small employers were unable to get loans and resorted to using credit cards to keep their businesses afloat.

The criticism from the small-business community grew louder as Obama released the details of his stimulus plan. Responding to the intense lobbying from that group, the Obama administration said it would use as much as $15 billion from the Troubled Asset Relief Program (TARP) to facilitate loans through the U.S. Small Business Administration (SBA).

Flying mostly under media radar, durable small companies that do everything from manufacturing forklift parts to specialty contracting have created the bulk of new jobs in recent years. Between 1994 through 2006, high-impact small businesses have accounted for 33.5 percent of employment growth for firms of their size. As defined by the SBA, these "high-impact" companies generally have fewer than twenty employees, are 25 years old or less, and represent about 3 percent of all firms. In contrast, during the same period, firms with 500 employees or more accounted for most of the job losses in the U.S. economy.

While business page headlines announced massive cutbacks at large U.S. multinational companies, small firms have been better employment generators in recent years. Even in the recession year of 2007, when housing starts declined 56.4 percent, 74 percent of the net new jobs in the economy were created by businesses with fewer than 500 employees. The number in incorporated self-employment rose to nearly 6 million in 2007, up from 5.5 million in 2006.

Helping the Small Business Survive

There is something glamorous about the idea of a couple of bright souls in an American basement or garage. They tinker around a bit, apply their imagination and creativity to a project, and—*voila!*—they become the next Steve Jobs or Bill Gates, reinventing the way the world works. Are those days over? Can America still foster the culture of innovation that helped it launch the second Industrial Revolution, land on the moon, and seed the Information Age? Will the next new wave of progress gush forth from alternative energy, nanotechnology, and biomedical advances? What would it take to end the Earth-killing carbon era and transform our economy according to President Obama's "Green Deal"?

Giving tax breaks to shop owners, contractors, and small manufacturers is the essence of bottom-up economics. "Trickle-up" or "bottom-up" policies provide more viable economic incentives than their obverse of supply-side economics. Bottom-up economics assumes that lower- and middle-class people eventually create jobs because they want to escape corporate salary stagnation and "cube life." They also want to invent things, offer new services, or fill a niche. This principle worked for people such as Samuel F. B. Morse, Thomas Edison, Lee DeForest, and thousands of other entrepreneurs who will never enjoy the kind of tax benefits that today's modern corporations enjoy.

Those who leave the corporate world do not always succeed in entrepreneurship, of course. Most fail. Yet those who make it generate employment, pay taxes, and anchor communities—in many cases much more so than multinational corporations. They can also be hypersuccessful like Bill Gates or Warren Buffett, who arguably became the most influential philanthropists on the planet after they donated their fortunes to solve such global problems as malaria, access to clean water, and education.

The wealth that springs from entrepreneurs becomes capital that enriches society. Libraries are built. Universities are funded. Diseases are cured. As a society, we should do our utmost to help give them a leg up. The great marketplace will decide whether or not their ideas or inventions are worth buying. As taxpayers, it empowers everyone to give them a chance. For the handful who can give back to their communities, country, or world, they give back in spades and create employment.

Freeing Up Credit

When you look at small-business growth, it is impossible to paint a rosy future without making available ample credit. The engines of job creation cannot function without bank loans. If a local machine shop cannot go to a community banker and borrow funds to expand its operation, then the owner will not be able to hire more people and sell to new markets. The credit crunch of 2008–2009 imperiled small-business owners most severely, which posed an ongoing problem for the global financial system at large.

Senator John Kerry (D-Massachusetts), who was chairman of the Committee on Small Business and Entrepreneurship in 2008, said the credit crisis was "preventing many small-businesspeople from getting the financing necessary to start or grow their businesses. Yet investment in small business can assist growth, since for every $33,000 loaned, one job is created or retained."

Some help is on the way. Venture capitalist and entrepreneur Karen Mills was confirmed in early April to head the SBA and promptly picked her management team. One of her first acts was to expand eligibility for the agency's 7(a) loan program, which would allow more businesses to qualify for government loans through September 30, 2010.

Linking to the Green Deal

Entrepreneurship and the green-collar economy go hand in hand. You cannot have innovation in environmental technologies without guys and gals in garages tinkering around. Economic incentives that flow into the green-collar sector also feed all construction, engineering, and technical trades. Houses and buildings will need to be programmed for energy savings. Solar appliances will need installers to put them on rooftops. Somebody will have to run the numbers to see how much money is being saved on utility bills. The opportunities to build entirely new businesses around environmental technology are endless.

The environmental technology industry is far more optimistic than Obama when it comes to job creation. They make the president look conservative on his estimates if everything comes together to fuel a green economy. According to the American Solar Energy Society (I am a former member), as many as 37 million jobs could be created by 2030 in the renewable energy and energy-efficiency industries. Currently, these businesses employ slightly fewer than 10 million workers but contribute $1 billion in revenue.

TAX CREDITS

What Was Promised: Obama promised to provide a new temporary tax credit to companies that create jobs in the United States. During 2009 and 2010, existing businesses would receive a $3,000 refundable tax credit for each additional full-time employee hired. For example, if a company originally has ten U.S. employees and increases its domestic full-time employment to twenty employees, then the company would get a $30,000 tax credit—enough to offset the entire added payroll tax costs to the company for the first $50,000 of income for the new employees. The tax credit was to benefit all companies creating net new jobs, even those struggling to make a profit. In addition, Obama promised to provide a $500 "making work pay" tax credit to almost every worker in America. Because self-employed small-business owners pay both the employee and the employer side of the payroll tax, this measure would reduce the burdens of this double taxation.

Stimulus Funds That Will Boost Green Businesses

The stimulus program will benefit specialized contractors in the building trades, alternative power, and energy efficiency. Although the initial plan will not be a substitute for a comprehensive climate-change policy, national green-building standards, or a renewable-energy-portfolio mandate (required use of clean energy by a certain date), it will likely seed thousands of businesses and create jobs. Here is a sampling of some programs that may benefit small firms:

- $6 billion for innovative-technology loan guarantees for electricity generation and renewable projects such as wind and solar power;
- $5 billion for weatherization assistance for low-income residents;
- $3.2 billion for energy-efficiency and conservation grants;
- $2 billion in grant funding for advanced battery systems to make them lighter and allow them to store more power over time; and
- $4.8 billion for other energy-efficiency programs such as energy-efficient federal vehicles and "greening" federal buildings.

What Congress Passed: Weeks before Obama took office, congressional leaders bristled at the idea of a new jobs credit; as a result, this was one of the first incentives to be axed. Since the majority of the tax incentives focused on tax cuts, short-term aid, and infrastructure projects, there was little left for small businesses, which came out as the biggest losers in this round, at least in terms of direct aid. However, Congress did pass alternative tax credits as a hiring incentive. Under the new plan, employers can receive a tax credit of 40 percent of the first $6,000 in wages for hiring unemployed veterans and "disconnected youth," defined as anyone between ages 16 and 25 who has not worked or attended school in the previous six months.

SMALL-BUSINESS EXPENSE LIMITS

What Was Promised: Obama promised to raise the small-business investment expensing limit to $250,000 through the end of 2009; this would give small businesses an additional incentive to make investments and start creating jobs. The February 2008 stimulus bill increased maximum Section 179 expenses to $250,000 but this expired in December 2008. This provision would encourage all firms to pursue investment through the end of 2009, but would particularly benefit small firms which generally have smaller amounts of annual property purchases and so choose to expense the cost of their acquired property. Essentially, these breaks allow businesses to write off the purchase of new equipment and extend the incentives offered during the Bush years.

What Congress Passed: Extension of Capital Expenditures. The stimulus package extended the capital expenditures write-off through 2009.

CAPITAL GAINS TAXES

What Was Promised: Obama promised to eliminate all capital gains taxes on investments made in small and start-up businesses. He also said he wanted to cut taxes for the small businesses that are creating jobs but struggling with restricted access to credit and skyrocketing costs for health care and energy.

What Congress Passed: Gains Exclusions. Under the congressional plan, people who hold certain small-business stock for at least five years can exclude 75 percent of the gains from federal taxes, compared with 50 percent previously. The break is limited to ten times the taxpayer's basis in the stock, or $10 million, depending on which is greater.

PUBLIC-PRIVATE BUSINESS INCUBATORS

What Was Promised: Obama promised to support entrepreneurship and spur job growth by creating a national network of public-private business incubators. These incubators would help entrepreneurs create start-up companies. Obama promised to invest $250 million per year to increase the number and size of incubators in disadvantaged communities throughout the country.

What Congress Passed: Congress did not address this initiative in the recovery act. A similar incentive was proposed in the 2010 budget to spur regional economic development and new businesses through $50 million in grants to the Economic Development Administration. A social-innovation fund was also proposed in the budget that would "test new approaches to major challenges, leveraging private and foundation capital to meet these needs and scaling up research-proven programs." This would be part of an initiative (again in the budget) to create 250,000 national and community service positions.

ADDITIONAL INCENTIVES

The stimulus law also reduced estimated tax payments from small businesses for the 2009 tax year and reduced the holding period to avoid gains from a Subchapter S corporation conversion from ten years to seven years. Also, even though it was not part of the stimulus legislation, the Obama administration said it would spend as much as $15 billion from TARP funds to help small businesses obtain loans, essentially buying loans from lenders. The administration also promised to extend $28 billion in SBA loan guarantees through the 2010 budget.

Who Benefits Most?

There is little doubt that the stimulus package will be the largest portion of seed money ever devoted to remaking the economy in a more sustainable mold. Provided the general economy does not collapse, there will be reasons to be optimistic about the green sector. The renewable energy and energy-efficiency industry grew three times faster (in terms of revenues) than the general economy in 2007.

By creating jobs that cannot easily be outsourced, the green-energy boom buoys states that have already embraced alternative power such as California, Oregon, Colorado, and Washington. Although solar panels were invented in the U.S., in 2008, the biggest consumer of solar panels in the world was Germany, which had a long-term tax incentive program in place for residents and businesses to buy and install them.

Though there is high potential for growth in green-collar jobs, these positions will never grow substantially without a comprehensive change in our energy policy. The changes would have to include the following: funding a digital smart grid long term to get energy from suppliers to consumers more efficiently, thereby saving energy; providing net metering, which gives credits to consumers who produce their own renewable energy; a national renewable-energy standard (Al Gore would like to see all electricity generated from renewable sources by 2030); job training in green-energy fields; and national building mandates that direct owners to do energy-efficient retrofits.

Small businesses buying green equipment get some relief in this package, although it is only slightly more than what was already on the books, and the tax write-off will not create additional jobs. Those businesses selling stock in their companies get a better break—provided they can sell for a profit during a recession.

Those in the construction businesses will not necessarily see much of a boost from Obama's small-business provisions, although the infrastructure and green-jobs components promise a boon for contractors of all sizes, depending on the types of projects. Small-business owners who are fortunate enough to sell their companies at a profit (assuming they had owned stock in them) will also owe less to Uncle Sam. The loss carryback provision is an accounting aid that will help businesses write off losses over a longer period.

There are myriad opportunities for business start-ups who hire veterans and the curious category of "disconnected" youths. Building a business around the Green Deal (see Chapter 4) will involve

Hottest Small-Business Opportunities Under Obamanomics

- Accounting and auditing
- Construction, fabrication, building management
- Electrical contracting
- Energy analysts
- Energy systems installation (solar, wind, geothermal)
- Mechanical, chemical, environmental, civil engineering
- Welding

some planning and education. You may need to become certified in green-building or green-auditing techniques. It's too soon to tell if the bidding process for the funded projects will protect small and minority-owned businesses.

Although the Obama plan will not directly affect the number of new business start-ups (around 600,000 annually), it may spur new growth in companies specializing in creating a green building industry. Even traditional jobs (see the following box) will flourish if Obamanomics funds a multiyear boom in construction, rehabilitation, or maintenance.

What Needs to Be Done?

Like a jigsaw puzzle, several pieces need to be in place before you can see the whole picture. Freeing up low-cost credit is essential; the lack of it has hurt small businesses disproportionately. Thousands of entrepreneurs who have been frozen out of loans or lines of credit at banks have resorted to loading up debt on high-interest credit cards.

Creating an infrastructure of assistance is another piece to help entrepreneurs. One of the best ways of creating this pro-entrepreneurial system is to examine what states have done to foster small-business growth. An excellent, comprehensive study by Robert Litan at the Kauffman Foundation in Kansas City lays out each element of a nurturing business climate.

Litan and the foundation created what they call a "State New Economy Index" that annually rates every state on how well it supports the creation of a knowledge-based, information-oriented business climate. The best environments, in the foundation's view, increase productivity through knowledge, globalization, entrepreneurship, and information technology. It's not just a handful of high-tech industries that benefit from these attributes; Litan extends his evaluation to health care, education, government, and real estate. When the best principles of the new economy are in place, every industry or sector can become more productive.

With its abundance of higher-education institutions and research and high-tech companies, Massachusetts led the survey overall in 2008, 2007, 2002, and 1999. Washington, Maryland, Delaware, and New Jersey round out the top five, while sixteen of the worst twenty states are located in the Great Plains, Deep South, and Midwest. What does Litan look for? He scores each state based on twenty-nine indicators, including some of the following:

- a high concentration of managers, professionals, and college-educated residents working in "knowledge jobs";

- companies that sell to global markets;

- above-average levels of entrepreneurship;

- states at the forefront of the information technology and Internet revolutions;

- institutions and residents that are highly connected to the digital economy;

- infrastructure that supports technological innovation; and

- domestic and foreign immigrants who are highly mobile and highly skilled knowledge workers who seek good employment opportunities and a good quality of life.

On that last item, it should be noted that there are thousands of qualified engineers, academics, researchers, and entrepreneurs who are in legal limbo because of antiquated U.S. immigration laws.

Although Obama did not overtly mention immigration in his economic plan, it is an unavoidable component to creating new businesses and jobs. Despite all that has happened to our economy in the past two years, smart, business-oriented people still want to come here and make a living. Barriers should be removed that prevent them from enjoying the American dream. Litan said that some 25 percent of high-tech start-ups are done by immigrants.

A central tenet of Obama's plan supports the technology-driven objective of the Kauffman study: broadband distribution and an updated grid. The top five states in the Kauffman survey all have extensive broadband access. States with high-speed Internet allow businesses to be situated in nearly every location; these businesses can also easily migrate to places where land prices and workers are more affordable (which, unfortunately, sometimes means offshore).

Updated electrical infrastructure also makes a clean-energy system a reality. As *Scientific American* wrote in an editorial on inauguration day, "The grassroots adoption of solar, wind, geothermal and other clean power is stifled by the grid's inefficiency at handling highly variable inputs and transmitting power over long distances. An investment in a [twenty-first century] grid would encourage energy reform without particularly favoring any specific production technology."

Where would the Obama administration start in this grassroots revolution? Developing a smart grid would lay the foundation. Afterward, the administration could offer every home and building owner a generous bucket of tax incentives and grants over the next decade. Denis Hayes, one of the cofounders of Earth Day, suggests the United States could "sensibly spend $6,000 per house increasing the energy efficiency of 50 million homes."

Small businesses would blossom under an ambitious green-retrofit program. Local businesspeople could set up shop doing weatherizing, setting up solar systems, or installing whole-house smart-energy networks. If the government can spend $110 billion to bail out dying carmakers that are building jalopies that few people want to buy, then it can take a plunge on the green-collar economy. Green businesses could be the next big small-business idea, and they could thrive in every community.

Manufacturing in the clean-energy sector could also experience a revival, provided the Obama administration ensures that U.S.-based makers of energy-efficient equipment can retool and have enough access to credit to make needed capital expenditures. Otherwise, this business could be shipped overseas. The manufacturing sector is in need of a revival. Since 2001, more than 4 million jobs have evaporated in the sector. Because it is unlikely that Detroit will move to create clean-energy cars any time soon (if it does at all), small shops could build or convert vehicles to electric, fuel-cell, or natural-gas engines. In addition, building the smart grid will require tremendous capacity for making electrical equipment, programming software, and even moving earth. All of those industries, in every community, could share in an entrepreneurial boom.

Information- and knowledge-friendly environments also create positive climates for other industries. Health care has improved in states that do not ban electronic prescriptions, according to the Kauffman study. Schools that are wired for broadband can better prepare their students for knowledge-based jobs. Green technology and manufacturing can flourish alongside non-smokestack industries.

Another piece of the puzzle has to be cost-effective universal health care. Some of the smartest, most ambitious people will not leave their corporations to start their own companies because they are worried about losing their health-care and retirement benefits. They have families to protect and retirements to fund through a system where they are mostly on their own with awful 401(k) plans. They could gain the flexibility and protection to start their own companies if both medical coverage and retirement plans were portable, affordable, and universal. Without a safety net, few people will take to the high wire of greater opportunities. The 2010 budget lays out the fiscal groundwork for affordable health care.

An even more radical approach to seeding small-business growth would be to cut payroll taxes. The self-employed, for example, pay both halves of federal, state, Social Security, and Medicare tax contributions. Litan, who was a member of Obama's transition team, suggests a national consumption tax to replace payroll levies. "You want more start-up job creation? Don't tax them," he notes.

Obama's team needs to be far more forward thinking if it's to lay down the roots of the green-tech revolution. They should look at what the Japanese, Germans, and Danes have done in terms of institutionalizing alternative energy and offering myriad incentives to green infrastructure. Think long term. Not one or two years, but twenty or thirty years. Make the Green Deal a generational project to address energy, environmental, population, urban growth, agricultural, and health concerns.

The American Recovery and Reinvestment Plan before Congress places a down payment on this economy. It will put 460,000 Americans to work with clean energy investments and double the capacity to generate alternative energy over the next three years. It will lay down 3,000 miles of transmission lines to deliver this energy to every corner of our country. It will save taxpayers $2 billion a year by making 75 percent of federal buildings more efficient. And it will save working families hundreds of dollars on their energy bills by weatherizing 2 million homes.

—President Barack Obama, January 26, 2009

CHAPTER 4

Job Creators and the Green-Collar Bonus

From the bleachers in a high school in Elkhart, Indiana, someone yelled for President Obama to create new jobs. The chief executive had left the corrosive atmosphere of Washington to stump for his plan as the U.S. Senate mulled it over.

"If we don't act immediately," Obama told more than 2,500 Elkhart citizens, where 15 percent unemployment ravaged the local economy, "unemployment across the country will rise, and our nation will slip into a crisis that, at some point, we may be unable to reverse."

Was the economy truly at the tipping point on that day, February 9, 2009, when Obama made his speech on the eve of the unveiling of his proposed bank bailout? There was little question that the once-robust jobs machine was running backward. More than 600,000 people became unemployed in the previous and following months (through April) and 500,000 the month before that. If Obama was to brake the worst recession since the 1930s, he needed not only to win over recalcitrant senators but also to persuade jobless workers in the recreational vehicle capital of the United States that he could get them back on the job.

Guided by a template drafted by the liberal Center for American Progress in 2008 titled "How to Spend $350 Billion in a First Year of Stimulus and Recovery," Obama's massive Green Deal addresses unemployment, the country's aging infrastructure, and environmental concerns all at once. Unlike the bailout packages passed by Congress in mid- and late 2008, the Obama plan seeks to spread federal spending across nearly every state in a variety of industries. It is a pragmatic and active government job-retention and job-creation program on a scale not seen since the Works Progress Administration.

Much of what Obama proposed during the campaign has broad support among those who criticized the lack of infrastructure investment over the past generation. The electrical grid is prone to breakdowns and blackouts, especially during the hot summer months. There is no way of getting power precisely to where it is needed. In an information era in which homes have more computers than televisions, fixing the grid is an essential item. Broadband connects everyone who has it to the global network.

Rebuilding roads and bridges is also high on most state wish lists, particularly after the catastrophic and deadly collapse of an interstate bridge in Minneapolis in 2007. And nearly all cities from New York to Chicago are hard pressed to keep their ancient mass-transit systems in decent repair.

Obama also placed energy and environmental priorities in the context of global competitiveness:

> We know the country that harnesses the power of clean, renewable energy will lead the twenty-first century, and yet it is China that has launched the largest effort in history to make their economy energy efficient. We invented solar technology, but we have fallen behind countries like Germany and Japan in producing it. New plug-in hybrids roll off our assembly lines, but they will run on batteries made in Korea. Well I do not accept a future where the jobs and industries of tomorrow take root beyond our borders—and I know you don't either. It is time for America to lead again.
>
> —President Obama, February 24, 2009

What makes Obama's plan so politically savvy is that he has wrapped a green ribbon around it. Informed by groups such as the Apollo Alliance and Green for All, he has championed the idea that there is no reason why environmentally sound projects cannot *also* be big job producers. Inner-city residents could learn new skills while weatherizing buildings. Installation of solar appliances, windmills, and geothermal heating systems also requires workers with new training and updated skills. The horrific energy-price increases of mid-2008 were still fresh in peoples' memories during his campaign: $4-a-gallon gasoline and $140-a-barrel crude-oil prices. Energy costs ravaged the economy. Everything from an airline ticket to a home-cleaning service rose in cost.

Although the recession knocked down crude prices to below $40 a barrel and gasoline to less than $2 a gallon, it was only a matter a time before these commodities would once again cripple family budgets. Natural gas prices for home heating, for example, did not ease during the severe winter of 2008–2009, when record cold and snow swept most of the eastern United States. Americans needed a break from the constant worries over energy bills and the political mumblety-peg of buying energy from countries that hate us and fund terrorism. Obama played on this fear effectively and sculpted it into a win-win jobs program for as many as 3 million workers.

The Green, Digital Economy

Heavily touting his green mission during the campaign and through-out his wrestling match with Congress over the economic stimulus legislation, Obama's team has a well-thought-out strategy in pushing for funding a "smart grid." As the backbone of the twenty-first century, this new way of managing, channeling, and distributing power is the key to greening America's power supplies.

Under the outdated model first put in place by Chicago utilities baron Sam Insull in the early twentieth century, large, central power stations fed electrons into a grid. At first, only communities within a certain radius of the power plant would consume the electricity, which often replaced smaller municipal or even residential generators. Once Insull wired entire communities, he created what he called "natural monopolies" that enabled him to lower the price of power because of economies of scale (see my book *Merchant of Power*). With the back-ing of President Herbert Hoover and the country's business interests, by the early 1930s Insull had managed to expand the "superpower" system of a multistate grid. Electricity generated in Indiana would serve Illinois customers, for example. The interconnections then provided regional and pooled power for an increasing number of customers coast to coast, fulfilling Insull's prediction that a "gospel of consumption" would create more power users from the cities to rural areas.

Insull and other power barons controlled their empires through vast, incredibly complicated holding companies, many of which collapsed after the 1929 crash because they were only capitalized by cross-ownership in the stocks of other holding companies. Decrying the failure of "the Insull monstrosity" in a 1932 campaign speech, Franklin D. Roosevelt and Congress broke up the tightly controlled utilities pyramids through the Public Utility Holding Company Act of 1935, which was effectively repealed in February 2006. Despite the splintering of the utility combines into hundreds of smaller companies, the old Insull grid system remained in place and is ill-suited for the needs of an information economy. It's a "dumb" entity that is prone to massive failure because it cannot automatically balance or send power where and when it's needed.

If Congress succeeds in seeding a massive conversion to renewable energy—which will take years—the old grid will not help much at all. Most of the largest sources of solar and wind energy (in the desert, Southwest, and Great Plains) are not close to power lines. You cannot feed renewable power into the grid without a means of getting it there. Even if there were power lines sitting in the middle of the best wind and solar corridors, the existing grid would not be able to adequately balance the surges coming from these renewable sources. By "digitizing" the grid, power would automatically move to where it is needed. Massive computer systems would be the electrical traffic cops. You could have power flowing from the sunny Western states while the East Coast was entering darkness.

The smart grid would also have a feedback mechanism for every user, so users could see how much energy they were using at any given point in the day. Traditionally, power is cheaper at night, when less electricity is being consumed. If you know when the lowest rates are available, you could set your major appliances to run at those times, cutting quite a bit off your electric bill. But because the old system (which is regulated by state utilities commissions based on the Insull model) is based on locking in profit by selling ever more power, there is no way you can precisely take advantage of the best rates.

"There's no way we can reach aggressive targets of 50 percent to 80 percent renewable electricity without a fully smart grid," reports New Energy Finance, an international research firm. "You can feed a few percent of renewable energy into the current grid without too many problems; go beyond that, however, and the network becomes unstable."

Under the new model of the "digi-grid," power consumers can become *prosumers*, in the words of Alvin Toffler. Say you wanted to install photovoltaic panels on your roof or a windmill in your backyard to produce energy. A smart grid would allow you to pump power back into the grid so that you receive either a credit on your electric bill—or a check. Theoretically, nearly every property can become a power producer. None of this is possible, though, without "smart metering" and a grid that knows what to do with hundreds of thousands of buildings that are suddenly two-way circuits; it is not possible to boost the renewable generating capacity efficiently without completely updating the grid.

In a January 2009 speech, Obama said modernizing the electrical grid will result in more than 3,000 miles of new or modernized transmission lines and 40 million smart meters in American homes. His aim is to double renewable-energy capacity between 2009 and 2011, but without some radical changes and long-term investment in the system over decades, Obama's goal is a pipe dream. The building of the digi-grid needs to continue well beyond his stimulus plan and first budgets.

If Obama succeeds in digitizing the electricity grid, it would revolutionize the way power is produced, priced, and distributed. Large commercial or office facilities could generate their own power, store it, and use it when needed. Homeowners and commercial and industrial property managers could offset their utility bills and dramatically reduce ownership costs. Solar-heating and geothermal units would even produce heat during the winter months. Fewer coal-burning or nuclear power plants would be needed. Climate change and air and water pollution could be reduced if distributed power become available on a large scale. Developing countries could adopt the renewable-energy model and technologies. The benefits to society and the planet would be enormous, although the obstacles would be daunting. Here is a sketch of what needs to happen to make the smart grid possible:

- **U.S. utilities would have to change how they are compensated.** Right now, the formula is simple. If a state commission regulates a utility, it grants rate approvals and locks in profits and dividends. Under this model, the more power the utility sells, the more money it (and its investors) make. This is why utilities have been such a safe investment over the years. Dividends generally rise and are consistently paid, regardless of the prevailing economic climate. But if the grid model changes, utilities would have to pay *customers* for reducing their energy use by producing their own power.

- **Microgrids would be created.** If the grid conversion is successful and millions of buildings start producing their own power, then big multibillion-dollar power plants would not be necessary. "Three-fourths of U.S. residential and commercial customers use electricity now at an average rate that does not exceed 1.5 and 12 kilowatts (thousands of watts), respectively, whereas a single conventional central power plant produces about a million kilowatts," according to the energy think tank Rocky Mountain Institute in its *Small Is Profitable: The Hidden Economic Benefits of Making Electrical Resources the Right Size.* Smaller is better, cleaner, and greener, but numerous federal and state laws (including the U.S. tax code) need to change to make this possible.

- **Your own power plant will be possible.** Provided that everyone from the IRS to the local power company is on board with the comprehensive smart-grid conversion and is willing to subsidize its start-up, there is no reason why consumers cannot power their entire homes and charge all-electric vehicles from their personal electrical supply using a combination of solar, wind, fuel cells, and batteries. This can be possible through cooperation on every level of government, a reduction in the cost of energy-producing equipment, and generous tax incentives.

♦ **Oil imports would be reduced.** A smarter grid powered by more renewable sources means cutting imported oil, which supplies more than two-thirds of our energy needs. A substantial portion of the nation's transportation fleet could be converted to plug-in electric and hybrid power. Approximately 20 percent of the nation's power could be supplied through a wind corridor that runs from Canada to Texas.

ADVANCED MANUFACTURING FUND

What Was Promised: Obama promised to create an advanced manufacturing fund to identify and invest in the most compelling advanced manufacturing strategies. The fund would have a peer-review selection and award process based on the Michigan 21st Century Jobs Fund.

What Congress Passed: This specific item did not make it into the stimulus plan.

MANUFACTURING EXTENSION PARTNERSHIP

What Was Promised: Obama promised to double funding for the Manufacturing Extension Partnership, which works with manufacturers across the country to improve efficiency, implement new technology, and strengthen company growth. This program, which had its funding slashed by the Bush administration, has engaged in more than 350,000 projects across the country; in 2006 alone, it helped create and protect more than 50,000 jobs.

What Congress Passed: Congress did not increase funding for the Manufacturing Extension Partnership in the stimulus plan or budget.

CLEAN-ENERGY INVESTMENTS

What Was Promised: Obama promised to invest $150 billion until 2019 to do the following: promote biofuels and fuel infrastructure; commercialize plug-in hybrids; promote the development of commercial-scale renewable energy; invest in low emissions coal plants; begin transitioning to a new, digital, electricity grid; and invest in job training to ensure American workers have the skills and tools they need to pioneer the first wave of green technologies. These reforms would double renewable-energy capacity from 2009 to 2011, enough to power 6 million homes. Modernizing the electricity grid would result in more than 3,000 miles of new or modernized transmission lines and 40 million smart meters in American homes. ·

What Congress Passed: Congress allocated $41 billion for energy-efficiency grants, advanced battery development, weatherization, electrical grid modernizations, and energy research (which wasn't all devoted to energy). This was largely seen as seed money for Obama's most high-profile energy projects, which will cost more than $100 billion. Some $4.5 billion was in the stimulus plans for the smart grid alone.

JOB TRAINING FOR CLEAN TECHNOLOGIES

What Was Promised: Obama promised to create job-training programs for clean technologies. This plan would increase funding for federal workforce training programs and direct these programs to incorporate training in green technologies such as advanced manufacturing and weatherization. Obama and Biden also promised to create an energy-focused youth-jobs program to invest in disconnected and disadvantaged youth.

What Congress Passed: Funding for Job Training. Congress passed $4 billion for job training for adults and youths. However, it was not clear whether these funds would be entirely dedicated to green jobs.

NEW ENERGY POLICIES

What Was Promised: Obama promised to create new federal policies and expand existing ones that have been proven to create new American jobs. He proposed a federal renewable portfolio standard that will require that 25 percent of American electricity be derived from renewable sources by 2025. He also promised to extend the Production Tax Credit (a tax break), which American farmers and investors used successfully to increase renewable-energy production and create new local jobs.

What Congress Passed: Extension of Tax Credit. Congress extended the Production Tax Credit to December 31, 2012, and provided for a 2.1-cent per kilowatt-hour income-tax credit for wind-produced electricity from utility-scale turbines. Neither the stimulus plan nor budget mentioned a portfolio standard, although it may come up in future energy or climate-change legislation.

CLEAN-ENERGY FINANCE INITIATIVE

What Was Promised: Obama promised to launch a clean-energy finance initiative to leverage $100 billion in private sector clean-energy investments from 2009 to 2012. Under this plan, the finance authority would provide loan guarantees and other financial support to help ease credit constraints for renewable-energy investors and catalyze new private-sector investment over the next three years.

What Congress Passed: New Incentives. Congress created a raft of incentives for clean-energy producers, including the following: a 30 percent investment tax credit for all renewable-energy producers (this was previously restricted to a select group); a Treasury Department grant program for renewable-energy facilities; a 50 percent credit for alternative-fuel pumps at gas stations through 2010, compared with a 30 percent credit under the old law; $2 billion in advanced energy-manufacturing credits; and a credit for plug-in electric vehicles ($2,500 minimum). Congress approved $1.6 billion in clean-energy bonds for facilities for wind, closed- and open-loop biomass, geothermal, small irrigation, hydropower, landfill gas, marine renewable, and trash combustion. Congress also approved $6 billion in temporary loan guarantees for renewable-energy power- and transmission-system projects that begin construction by September 20, 2011.

WEATHERIZING HOMES AND BUILDINGS

What Was Promised: Obama promised to save low-income families an average of $350 per year by weatherizing homes. He also promised to modernize 75 percent of federal building space, saving taxpayers $2 billion per year in lower federal energy bills. As of 2009, the U.S.

federal government is the world's largest consumer of energy. The recovery and reinvestment plan will save taxpayer dollars and help catalyze a green building industry.

What Congress Passed: Weatherization Upgrades. Congress approved $5 billion in weatherization grants for low- and moderate-income families to help lower utility bills. Congress also approved $4.2 billion in energy-efficiency upgrades in public housing and federal buildings.

ADDITIONAL INCENTIVES PASSED

High-Speed Rail. Congress approved investments of $16.4 billion in public transit and high-speed rail. This is a first step to reducing reliance on vehicular transportation, which is a huge contributor to pollution and global warming.

Waste Removal. Congress approved $6.2 billion for the environmental cleanup of former weapons-production plants, as well as for U.S. Environmental Protection Agency Superfund waste sites, which are toxic dumps that have not already been cleaned. Congress also approved $1.38 billion for loans and grants for rural waste disposal.

Congress also set aside the following: $2.5 billion for renewable-energy research and development, $2 billion for advanced battery manufacturing, and $400 million for Department of Defense energy and efficiency programs.

Who Benefits Most?

Nearly any firm involved in energy efficiency or renewable power will find it worthwhile to finance capital expenditures or research and development. The tax credits alone translate into the government picking up the cost of nearly one-third of most qualifying projects. These subsidies and grants could trigger a golden age in green energy if the breaks continue past 2011.

Buildings alone eat up huge amounts of energy, as much as one-third of the total consumption in the United States. However, the

National Association of Homebuilders estimates that green building could become a $70 billion industry by 2014.

All buildings, from mountain cabins to global corporate campuses, could become more energy efficient by producing their own power; this would boost corporate profits while trimming operating costs. Aging federal and public-housing buildings are good candidates for energy-efficiency upgrades. Although local contractors will get a portion of these dollars, the attention getters in this area are giants in power-related systems, such as the following companies: the General Electric Company (GE US); Siemens AG (SIE GY); ABB Limited (ABB); United Technologies (UTX); Ingersoll-Rand Company (IR); Johnson Controls Inc. (JCI); Cree, Inc. (CREE); Energy Focus Inc. (EFOI).

Having noted these companies, do not just pick one of them and assume that you will reap a windfall during Obama's term. It takes time for infrastructure funds to course through a $13 trillion–plus economy. Some technologies will gain acceptance in the marketplace, while others will fail. And energy systems rarely work with only one piece of equipment; they need a symphony of other systems and skilled professionals working together. You will also need to consider smaller companies that specialize in toxic-waste remediation (Superfund cleanups), railroad infrastructure, and anything to do with energy efficiency, particularly in buildings.

Making buildings efficient requires a comprehensive systems approach. Owners need to update heating and cooling systems, insulation, and lighting and controls. No single company can provide the whole solution. This is why a portfolio of these kinds of companies makes more sense than picking individual issues.

Think bottom-up economics in the Green Deal. Akin to what happened in Silicon Valley with information and computing technologies, many of the mainstream players may not have the best products, services, or ideas. The next billionaires may be working out of a tiny company or garage.

Again, the most prudent investment in the Obamanomics Green Deal is to avoid betting on a single company, technology, industry, or sector. There will be more losers than winners. Where can you find out-of-the-box thinkers and innovators who will do well under the Green Deal? You can get a global breadbasket through any world stock index fund, or you can cherry pick a "clean technology" approach through the Powershares WilderHill Progressive Energy Portfolio exchange-traded fund (PUW) or the First Trust Nasdaq Clean Edge U.S. Liquid Series Index Fund (QCLN).

I like diversifying through mutual or exchange-traded funds, but these have notable risks. For example, take the Powershares WilderHill Clean Energy Portfolio exchange-traded fund (PBW). The fund seems like the right vehicle if you are excited about the prospects of energy sources that do not produce carbon dioxide. It invests in a variety of stocks in the alternative-energy, semiconductor, electrical component, and related industries. However, it is not unusual for a small industry segment to be quite volatile. So why concentrate market risk in a handful of companies? Maybe major alternative-energy advances will come from the nanotechnology, biotechnology, or semiconductor industries. They may even come from electric utilities or major energy companies. Why narrow your bet to fewer than fifty stocks?

The predictable truth about investing is that you do not know where your best returns will come from, so why squeeze the field to a handful of stocks and pare your chances of finding a winner? This is why an alternative-energy or climate-change portfolio does not make better sense. You are better off investing in a broad-based index or exchange-traded fund that samples more than 500 stocks.

What Is Needed

The Green Deal is like an intricate machine: all the pieces have to come together at the right time for it to be a success. If there is a single part missing, it could be a disaster. The most important components of Obama's plan are the financing mechanisms and the political changes necessary for things such as the smart grid to become possible. One could argue that the program isn't ambitious enough.

Most of what survived the legislative process is merely a down payment on essential infrastructure upgrades. The grid-modernization project alone is estimated to cost $165 billion and could take a decade of software development, transmission-line extensions, and relaxing of federal regulations.

There is no shame in being even more audacious when it comes to remaking the energy economy. Green jobs groups such as Green for

Green Jobs in Highest Demand

- **Green building architects, consultants, and contractors.**
  If you happen to be looking for a new career, it would
  not hurt to be accredited through the U.S. Green Building
  Council's (www.USGBC.org) LEED program (Leadership in
  Energy and Environmental Design), which certifies buildings and neighborhoods on their environmental attributes.
  Any building or contracting firm can do green rehabbing
  with additional training. The number of LEED-certified
  buildings has grown as much as 700 percent annually
  since 1993, according to the building council. If the Green
  Deal succeeds on a large scale, it will employ millions in
  the building trades alone, perhaps offsetting the horren-
  dous job losses of the last several years.

- **Engineers, engineers, engineers.** Nearly every kind of
  engineer does well under the complete Obama Green
  Deal. Civil engineers will be needed to design and manage
  infrastructure projects such as rebuilding bridges, highways,
  tunnels, and sewer and water systems. Chemical and electrical engineers will be needed to design and build new battery and power systems. Software engineers will be needed
  to program the smart grid. Nanotechnology and biotechnology engineers will work on the latest solar-cell design or
  biofuel catalyst. The sky is the limit for this profession.

- **Building managers, facilities consultants, and energy
  auditors.** Green buildings require a specialized system
  that monitors energy use, especially if power is produced
  on-site. Every structure on the planet can be redesigned to
  save energy and resources, but it takes professionals with
  constantly updated training.

- **Project and program managers** (for all green-building
  and green-design projects)

- **Energy auditors** (to measure building energy use and waste)

- **Reliability engineers** (to design and monitor energy systems)

- **Sustainability analysts and auditors** (to determine how organizations will benefit from green projects)
- **Systems integrators** (to combine several energy and building systems)
- **Thin-films technologists** (for manufacturing solar cells)
- **Solar design and installation technicians**
- **Wind-power design and installation technicians**
- **Geothermal design and installation technicians**
- **Biological systems specialists** (to design, manage, and operate energy or biomass systems)
- **Environmental managers** (corporate positions in sustainability)
- **Green industrial designers**
- **Green interior designers**
- **Green landscapers and designers**
- **Auto retrofitters** (to convert gasoline or diesel engines to hybrids or electrics)
- **Lawyers** (environmental law specialists)
- **Urban planners** (specializing in smart growth and sustainable development)
- **Smart-home designers and technicians** (to design and install computer systems that network all appliances and energy systems)
- **Organic farmers**
- **Biomass energy specialists** (to generate energy from waste)
- **Cogeneration specialists** (to generate power from heating systems)
- **Microturbine specialists** (to generate power on-site from alternative sources)
- **Fuel-cell specialists**
- **Educators and trainers**
- **Green tourism agents and planners**
- **Tax planners and preparers** (specializing in green tax incentives)

All and the Apollo Alliance have lobbied for broad-based spending in renewable-energy and related job creation. By training people to do such things as energy rehabbing and alternative-energy production, leaders of the movement hope to alleviate the double-digit unemployment in inner-city communities. At the same time, their founders have envisioned a government program akin to the Apollo moon program in both scope and sheer ambition. Why not tap the Pentagon and the Department of Defense's Defense Advanced Research Projects Agency to fund projects for long-term battery storage, the electric grid, or all-electric, rechargeable vehicles? Wouldn't a smart, reliable grid improve national security?

Perhaps in later legislation, Congress may just create a permanent suite of tax incentives, as opposed to direct funding, to keep the Green Deal on track. If Obamanomics stays true to its social-capitalism mission, it may serve as a silent partner in the most ambitious objectives of the program. It can provide seed funding or tax incentives for the private sector while letting that sector take the risks.

While the administration is engaged in environmental job creation, it could overhaul the long-term financial and tax incentives for green building. Why not offer lower thirty-year mortgage rates (or guarantees) for all environmentally sound construction or rehabbing? The Federal National Mortgage Association (Fannie Mae) and the Federal Home Loan Mortgage Corporation (Freddie Mac)—assuming they can be reconstituted as entirely public guarantors of mortgages—could offer the discounts and guarantee the loans. The 2030 Challenge Stimulus Plan proposed by the Architecture 2030 organization suggests combining a mortgage buy-down program for "greened" residential and commercial buildings, which could result in more than 8 million jobs.

Fiscal conservatives object that such a massive project will require tax dollars for programs that will only benefit selected, well-heeled constituencies and lobbies. But a private-public partnership (perhaps using the clean-energy initiative as the vehicle) that functions more like a venture capital firm would be a better entity to dole out money than a handful of bureaucrats. Ultimately, the Green Deal could pay for itself without adding to the national debt.

In a global economy where the most valuable skill you can sell is your knowledge, a good education is no longer just a pathway to opportunity—it is a prerequisite. Right now, three-quarters of the fastest-growing occupations require more than a high school diploma. And yet, just over half of our citizens have that level of education. We have one of the highest high school dropout rates of any industrialized nation. And half of the students who begin college never finish.

—President Barack Obama, address to Congress, February 24, 2009

CHAPTER 5

Get Smarter

The acrid compromise that Obama reached in order to push his stimulus plan through the U.S. Senate carved billions out of the educational funding section of the bill. The original legislation set aside $150 billion for everything from preschool education to college grants. Though Congress only approved $100 billion, this amount still nearly doubled the budget of the Department of Education. In addition, the states still received some necessary emergency funding. Because the recession was devastating their tax revenues, the states were faced with laying off teachers and other public employees at the time the stimulus plan was first proposed. (Unlike the federal government, state legislatures must, by law, balance their budgets.) The Obama stimulus secured funding to keep states from firing hundreds of thousands of education professionals.

The stimulus package was originally supposed to be a long-needed construction boost for the nation's 97,000 public schools. Although the total requested allocation for school repair did not make it through the Senate, aging schools stood to gain enough money to create better learning environments.

In the original stimulus plan, which survived the House vote, Congress was to set aside about $120 billion for public-school infrastructure. Of this amount, $14 billion was to go toward fixing roofs and boilers, mending leaky windows, and updating buildings. In addition to educational benefits, this would create inner-city construction jobs; for every $1 billion spent on schools, it's estimated some 10,000 positions are created.

But Senate Republicans scaled back Obama's school-rebuilding component drastically in a deal to win enough votes for passage. Ultimately, the total package for local school districts amounted to $30 billion, although none of the funds were specifically targeted for school repairs. Although any education spending is welcome, it is estimated that as much as $360 billion will be needed to repair and modernize schools. Many schools cut their maintenance budgets as much as 12 percent during the Bush years to help meet Bush-era No Child Left Behind (NCLB) standards.

In his first full news conference in the White House on February 9, 2009, Obama lashed out at the GOP pushback: "When it comes to how we approach the issue of fiscal responsibility . . . it is a little hard for me to take criticism from folks about this recovery package after they presided over a doubling of the national debt. I am not sure they have a lot of credibility when it comes to fiscal responsibility."

Obama mounted an even more aggressive response after holding a fiscal responsibility summit a few weeks later on February 23 and in his address to Congress the following evening. He wanted to neutralize the idea that he would not trim the federal budget while he added bold new education programs: "In this budget, we will end education programs that do not work and end direct payments to large agribusinesses that do not need them," he said. "We will eliminate the no-bid contracts that have wasted billions in Iraq, and reform our defense budget so that we're not paying for Cold War–era weapons systems we don't use."

Using his bully pulpit to his eloquent advantage, Obama called for a reduction in high-school dropout rates, "the highest proportion of college graduates by 2020," and exhorted adults to "commit to at least one year or more of higher education or career training."

When you add up all of the programs, Obama's commitment to education may eclipse that of the GI Bill after World War II and touch every level of education from preschool through college. Unfortunately, most of Obama's comprehensive educational agenda was not addressed in the stimulus package.

Early Childhood Education

What Was Promised: Obama unveiled a comprehensive Zero to Five plan that would provide critical support to young children and their parents. Unlike other early childhood education plans, the Obama-Biden plan emphasized early care and education for infants, which is essential for children to be ready to enter kindergarten. Their plan would create early-learning challenge grants to help states move toward voluntary, universal preschool education. Obama also promised to quadruple Early Head Start funding, and increase Head Start support. Both programs are geared to help preschoolers in economically distressed neighborhoods. In addition, he promised to increase access to affordable and high-quality child care to ease the burden on working families.

What Congress Passed: Increased Funding. Congress approved about $2.1 billion for Head Start, Early Head Start, and related child care programs for the poor.

STATE FISCAL RELIEF

What Was Promised: Obama promised to provide $25 billion in state fiscal relief so that local governments do not have to decide between raising property taxes and cutting vital services. Obama said he hoped the funds would help states and localities continue to provide such essential services as health care, police, fire protection, and education without raising taxes or fees.

What Congress Passed: State Relief. In the stimulus package, the states received $55 billion to prevent layoffs and program cutbacks and to make some school repairs. Congress also approved $12 billion for special education. Much of this money aims to offset lost tax revenue.

REFORMING NO CHILD LEFT BEHIND

What Was Promised: Obama promised to reform No Child Left Behind so that teachers are not forced to spend the academic year preparing students to fill in bubbles on standardized tests. He also promised to improve the assessments used to track student progress to measure readiness for college and the workplace and improve student learning in a timely, individualized manner. Under the current law, all students must be at a specified national average for math and reading proficiency by 2014. During the Bush era, this meant reorienting most of public education toward regular testing and evaluation, although Congress never appropriated enough money to fully implement the program. As of April 2009, about 6,000 of the nation's 95,000 schools were believed not to comply with No Child Left Behind standards.

What Congress Passed: Congress did not take any action on No Child Left Behind in the stimulus plan or budget; it is to take up the issue of reauthorizing NCLB in late 2009. Early indications were that the Obama administration would maintain extensive testing to determine student competencies but would work with teachers and administrators to find a better way to evaluate student progress. The budget proposal is particularly vague on what the administration planned to do other than "helping states to develop high quality, rigorous standards and assessments, vigorously supporting and rewarding effective teaching, and investing in and widely disseminating effective approaches to improving student achievement to help all students make progress toward high standards." Comments from the Department of Education make it appear as though the administration would ask the states and governors to initiate many of the new standards. Yet questions remained. Would ineffective teachers be fired? How would they be evaluated? How would the best teachers be identified and rewarded? How would the powerful teachers' unions be involved?

SUPPORTING HIGH-QUALITY SCHOOLS AND CLOSING LOW-PERFORMING CHARTER SCHOOLS

What Was Promised: Obama promised to double funding for the federal charter school program to help create more charter schools.

The administration said it would provide this expanded charter school funding only to states that improve accountability for charter schools, allow for interventions in struggling charter schools, and have a clear process for closing down chronically underperforming charter schools.

What Congress Passed: Congress did not address this in the stimulus plan or in the 2010 budget.

IMPROVING MATH AND SCIENCE EDUCATION

What Was Promised: Obama promised to recruit graduates with math and science degrees to the teaching profession and to help teachers learn from professionals in the field.

What Congress Passed: Funding National Science Foundation. Under the stimulus plan, Congress provided the National Science Foundation with $60 million for the Noyce Teacher Scholarship program, $25 million for the math and science partnership, and $15 million for the science master's program.

ADDRESSING THE DROPOUT CRISIS

What Was Promised: Obama promised to invest in intervention strategies, such as personal academic plans, teaching teams, parent involvement, mentoring, intensive reading and math instruction, and extended learning time.

What Congress Passed: Congress did not address this issue in the stimulus plan.

AFTER-SCHOOL OPPORTUNITIES

What Was Promised: Obama promised to double funding for the main federal support for after-school programs, the 21st Century Community Learning Centers program, to serve 1 million more children.

What Congress Passed: Congress did not address this funding in the stimulus plan, but it did consider it in its budget outline for 2010.

COLLEGE OUTREACH

What Was Promised: Obama promised to support outreach programs such as GEAR UP (Gaining Early Awareness and Readiness for Undergraduate Programs), TRIO (programs for disadvantaged students), and Upward Bound (college-entrance support) to encourage more young people from low-income families to consider and prepare for college.

What Congress Passed: Congress did not address these programs in the stimulus plan, but it did increase funding to the Pell Grant program and Title I programs in primary schools by $17 billion and $20 billion, respectively.

SUPPORTING COLLEGE CREDIT INITIATIVES

What Was Promised: Obama promised to create a national Make College a Reality initiative to increase students taking advanced placement or college-level classes nationwide 50 percent by 2016. He also promised to build on his bipartisan proposal in the U.S. Senate to provide grants for students seeking college-level credit at community colleges if their schools do not provide those resources.

What Congress Passed: Congress did not address this issue in the stimulus plan.

SUPPORTING ENGLISH LANGUAGE STUDENTS

What Was Promised: Obama promised to support transitional bilingual education and to hold schools accountable for ensuring that students with limited English complete school.

What Congress Passed: Congress did not address this issue in the stimulus plan.

RECRUITING TEACHERS

What Was Promised: Obama promised to create new teacher service scholarships that will cover four years of undergraduate or two years of graduate teacher education, including high-quality alternative programs for midcareer recruits in exchange for teaching for at least four years in a high-need field or location.

What Congress Passed: AmeriCorps Funding. Congress provided an additional $200 million funding for AmeriCorps through the Corporation for National Community Service, a Clinton-era program that encourages students to become teachers in inner-city schools. In addition, the budget calls for expanding the program to 250,000 positions from 75,000 at the end of 2008. Teacher quality enhancement programs received $100 million from the stimulus package. In a separate measure, on April 22, the president signed into law a bill that sets aside $1.1 billion for AmeriCorps in 2009. Volunteers will be paid a stipend of $5,350. A Social Innovation fund to provide matching grants to nonprofits will receive $50 million.

PREPARING TEACHERS

What Was Promised: Obama promised to require that all schools of education be accredited. Obama and Biden also promised to create a voluntary national performance assessment to ensure that every new educator is trained and ready to walk into the classroom and start teaching effectively. Obama also promised to create teacher residency programs to supply 30,000 exceptionally well-prepared recruits to high-need schools.

What Congress Passed: Congress did not address this issue in the stimulus plan.

RETAINING TEACHERS

What Was Promised: Obama promised to expand mentoring programs that pair experienced teachers with new recruits. He also promised to provide incentives to give teachers paid common planning time so they can collaborate to share best practices.

What Congress Passed: Congress did not address this issue in the stimulus plan.

REWARDING TEACHERS

What Was Promised: Obama promised to promote new and innovative ways to increase teacher pay. Under his plan, districts would be able to provide a salary increase to accomplished educators who serve as mentors to new teachers as well as to teachers who consistently excel in the classroom. Districts can also reward teachers who work in underserved places such as rural areas and inner cities.

What Congress Passed: Though Congress did not address this issue in the stimulus plan or budget measures, Arne Duncan, the education secretary, said he would spend $5 billion from the stimulus funds for schools, colleges, and early childhood programs nationwide to prevent teacher layoffs, reduce class sizes, and revamp older schools.

MAKING COLLEGE AFFORDABLE

What Was Promised: Obama promised to make college affordable by creating a new American Opportunity Tax Credit. This universal and fully refundable credit would ensure that the first $4,000 of a college education is completely free for most Americans; it would cover two-thirds the cost of tuition at the average public college or university and make community-college tuition completely free for most students. Recipients of the credit would have to conduct 100 hours of community service.

What Congress Passed: College Affordability Credit. Congress renamed the Hope Scholarship the American Opportunity Tax Credit and raised the amount of the college tax break to as high as $2,500 a year from $1,800 a year. The credit could boost the amount of money you can claim only through 2010. Basically, you could claim more education-related expenses if your income is less than $160,000 for joint filers and $80,000 for singles and those who file separately. As much as 40 percent of the credit is refundable. In addition to the credit, Congress passed other financial aid incentives to make college more affordable. Congress raised the maximum amount of the Pell Grant from $4,360 to $5,350 per year in 2009 and to $5,550 in 2010 by setting aside an additional $16 billion for the program. It's estimated this will help 7 million students. The catch is that only low-income students and families qualify, so it's little help to the middle class.

SIMPLIFYING FINANCIAL AID

What Was Promised: Obama promised to eliminate the current federal financial aid application and to enable families to apply simply by checking a box on their tax forms; this authorizes a family's tax information to be used, eliminating the need for a separate application.

What Congress Passed: Congress did not address this issue in the stimulus plan.

SUPPORTING STUDENTS WITH DISABILITIES

What Was Promised: Obama promised to ensure the academic success of students with disabilities by enforcing and increasing funding for the Individuals with Disabilities Education Act (IDEA), and by holding schools accountable for providing students with disabilities with necessary services and support. Obama also promised to support early intervention services for infants and toddlers and to improve college opportunities for high school graduates with disabilities.

What Congress Passed: Funding for IDEA. Congress set aside $12.2 billion for the Individuals with Disabilities Education Act. Of that amount, $11.3 billion went directly to states, $400 million went to preschools, and $500 million went to grants for infants and toddlers. Congress did not address the other initiatives in the stimulus plan.

ADDITIONAL INCENTIVES PASSED

Federal Energy Research. Congress set aside about $4 billion for advanced energy research through the Department of Energy. Another $180 million was to be distributed through the National Institute of Standards and Technology to construct research facilities.

Medical Research. Some $10 billion was tabbed for biomedical research and facilities through the National Institutes of Health.

Computer Centers. Public libraries and community colleges would receive an additional $200 million for computer centers.

529 Plan Utilization. Congress loosened the rules for use of Section 529 college savings plan withdrawals, which are tax free if used for higher education. Now computer purchases will be allowed as "qualified expenses," meaning if you or your children must buy a laptop or desktop computer, then you can use 529 funds to pay for this equipment while avoiding tax on those withdrawals.

The Department of Education also received $100 million for "impact aid construction," $720 million for educational technology and education for homeless children, $680 million for vocational rehabilitation and independent living, and $310 million for statewide data systems and student aid administration.

Who Benefits Most?

Low-income families will benefit most from public-school support for early childhood education. The $13 billion targeted for Title I programs will have the greatest impact on impoverished students. The children's advocacy community, which had seen a 13 percent cut in inflation-adjusted funding for these programs during the Bush years, welcomed the increases for Head Start, Early Head Start, and child care for impoverished parents and children. If the money is efficiently spent, then 55,000 to 120,000 children will benefit. Approximately $2 billion will go to child care programs for working parents who make $21,000 a year or less (individually), and the remainder will go to Head Start programs, which focus on preschool children by providing them a safe environment and increased access to health and dental care.

Combined with the massive state fiscal-aid component of the stimulus plan that will help bolster school systems and the Medicaid program, the small amount set aside for early education will act as a modest antipoverty campaign. According to research from the National Head Start Association, society receives $9 in benefits for every dollar invested in Head Start children. Children from Head Start are likely to come out of the program with higher test scores, better vocabulary, and lower mortality rates. There is also a measurable impact in lowering crime rates. Although an estimated 110,000 additional children will gain access to Head Start under the stimulus plan, the total need is about 2 million (some 900,000 are served now), said Bill Bentley, chief executive of Voices for America's Children and one of the founders of the thirty-six organizations in the Children's Leadership Council coalition.

Teachers and other educational professionals across the country gain a short-term reprieve from some budget cuts. Because congressional negotiators struck the school-repair fund from the final legislation, the funds that remain for this purpose were contained in a broad-based $54 billion "fiscal stabilization" component. This means contractors specializing in school repairs would benefit, although not as much as they would have under the plan that passed the House.

Health-care students and inner-city teachers gain some support, as do biomedical and energy researchers in postgraduate environments.

College-aid students and families get some relief under the financial aid provisions, although the Obama plan does little, if anything, to reduce the overall cost of college or pare student debt in a meaningful way.

What Needs to Be Done?

The stimulus plan that emerged from Congress provided piecemeal funding for many of Obama's initiatives. His future budgets will likely seek to fill in the holes. Broader reforms could include the following suggestions, some of which have been brought forward by *Education Week* editors.

More Support for Struggling, Low-Income Students and Their High Schools. Obama's early childhood intervention programs may eventually help in many small ways, but little will change unless the worst schools and neighborhoods receive the same financial and educational support as the best schools. For that, the link between local property-tax revenue and money available for schools needs to be altered by diversifying tax-revenue sources. There is not much that the federal government can do to alleviate this inequality unless it dramatically increases the amount going to schools, which are largely funded by state and local taxes.

Reforming No Child Left Behind. Although public school teachers and administrators have been clamoring to reduce the burden of No Child Left Behind for years, it's difficult to say how the Obama administration will change this law to ensure accountability and adequate support funding. Millions of children from varying backgrounds cannot suddenly improve their math, reading, and other essential skills without additional support in the classroom, which NCLB does not directly provide. Many educators regarded NCLB as a hostile act during the Bush years, a cynical move to deprive schools of federal dollars while punishing mostly inner-city schools that failed to raise their test scores. After all, Congress laid the foundation for the program by ramping up testing but failed to fully fund the educational component or address the larger issue of changing inner-city educational environments.

Recruiting and Preparing More Teachers. Obama stressed account-ability for schools and teachers, so the real reforms lie ahead in future initiatives. His administration will need to learn how to keep the best teachers on the job and to give them more career flexibility; that may involve abolishing tenure or reforming certification standards. In most urban school districts, teachers are underpaid and overburdened. There needs to be a better way of training and rewarding the best teachers.

A Better Focus on Graduation Rates and College Readiness. There needs to be more emphasis on core courses and incentives to get students to graduate. To improve test scores and graduation rates, even extending the school day or year should be considered. Some of the most successful educational programs employ year-round schooling.

Improving College Affordability and Access. Each year, fewer Americans can afford a college education. On average, students come out of school with $20,000 in debt for each year in school. However, Obama's education changes will only help incrementally. Making more college grants (and tax breaks) available will largely help students in *community* colleges. At first blush, that's a great idea because junior colleges are some of the best, unsung bargains in higher education. Along these lines, combined curriculums for high school and college also help, allowing secondary students to earn college credit while still in high school. This can be done by promoting advanced placement tests where high-school students obtain college credit.

The Higher-Education Dilemma

Higher education for the middle class fared the worst in the legislation that emerged from Obama's stimulus package. The core problems

Education Items in Proposed Budget

The Obama administration was building on its campaign promises in its proposed 2010 budget outline. Here are some of the highlighted proposals for higher education:

- Change the Pell Grant program into a true entitlement by increasing the maximum amount to $5,550 in 2010–11 (up $200 from $5,350 in 2009–10) and indexing the maximum Pell Grant to inflation (consumer price index) plus 1 percent.
- Replace the federally guaranteed Federal Family Education Loan Program with 100 percent direct lending. This will save the government money and possibly lower interest rates while virtually eliminating private loans.
- Modernize the Perkins loan program so that campus-based, low-interest loans would be more widely available, overhauling the inefficient and inequitable current program.
- Provide about $2.5 billion (to 2015) for the Access and Completion Incentive Fund to "help low-income students succeed and complete their college education."
- Create a Promise Neighborhoods program to support children in high-poverty areas.
- Make the American Opportunity Tax Credit (formerly the Hope Scholarship) permanent.
- Triple the number of graduate science fellowships.
- Streamline the student-aid application process.

have been lack of financial support to get the most imperiled students through the system and the runaway cost of college tuition; families have not been able to keep up with it and have increasingly turned to loans, saddling both students and parents with college debt for years after students graduate. This has impaired the ability of young adults to save money, buy homes, and save for their own retirements. The recession also added to this misery as countless students put off going to college because of the devastating impact financial markets had on household incomes and savings.

However, demand is still high for college degrees. The College Board reports: "Family income rises with the educational attainment of the householder. For those with a bachelor's degree or more in 2007, the median income was $100,000, compared to $49,739 for those with a high school diploma and no college education."

As a result, the parents and children of baby boomers have fueled the demand for college degrees. After all, one of the main orthodoxies for success in American life—at least the ability to earn a decent salary—has been that a university diploma opens a lot of doors. And the better the college, the more employers are willing to pay a graduate. Corollary growth has been spurred in MBA programs and other graduate-level degrees. If you were an employer, whom would you pay the executive salary to—an employee with a BA from a state college or a "climber" with an MBA from Harvard, Wharton, or Kellogg? Name brands have considerable cachet in determining salary scales, and parents have been willing to pay top dollar just for the recognition that a top school brings a new graduate.

College is also more expensive because it is still a desirable way of getting ahead in an increasingly difficult financial climate. Like any other economic constant, in addition to other factors, steady demand has boosted its price. Average total charges at a private, four-year college were $34,132 for the 2008–09 school year, reports the College Board, with most of the top-tier schools costing more than $40,000 annually. Public universities averaged about $25,000.

What's telling, though, is not the actual "list prices" of universities, it's the fact that their bills have been outpacing inflation more than any other big-ticket item in the American economy. College bills rose more than 5 percent between 2007 and 2008. Consumer inflation was up only 0.10 percent during that period (mostly because of a recession). Generally, these expenses have outrun inflation by 1.2 to 2 times from 1958 through 2005, according to finaid.com, a financial aid service. If college inflation is averaging about 8 percent per year, it means the cost of higher education *doubles* every nine years. Worse yet, children born today would face a college bill that has tripled when they matriculate.

Even a modest state-school bachelor's degree costing $100,000 translates to a $300,000 price tag in the future. Clearly, the rate of increase in these expenses isn't sustainable for most families, and they plunge into debt to cover the tab. Unfortunately, the Obama education plan offered cold comfort to families facing ever-higher tuition bills. A bevy of credits and write-offs is loaded with exemptions based on income. Like most of the tax code, the IRS guide to education breaks is riddled with confusing language and far too many exclusions. As a result, most taxpayers don't take advantage of the education write-offs available (eighty-six pages' worth in IRS Publication 970, *Tax Benefits for Education,* in 2008).

Congress also needs to address the question of how best to provide low-cost, guaranteed federal college loans, which had been subsidized by the government and offered through private lenders. The Obama administration was fighting to make the entire program a direct-lending plan through the government. That would have lowered the cost of the loans because banks would not be able to make a profit, a lucrative business in past years. As this went to press, though, the financial services industry was fighting that proposal vigorously. With student debt topping $500 billion in 2008, an amount that has tripled since 1983, the need to reduce students' burdens entering the workforce was a national priority. The Administration also hoped to expand Pell Grant and Perkins loan amounts.

The most rational approach for higher education would be to offer one annual blanket credit for education for at least $10,000. Washington could also wield a big stick with research institutions by withholding federal research dollars if a college does not provide a certain percentage of grant aid to underclass students. Until then, the tax code will continue to be a bewildering hodgepodge that most parents will ignore.

I know that some are skeptical about the size and scale of this recovery plan. I understand that skepticism, which is why this recovery plan must and will include unprecedented measures that will allow the American people to hold my administration accountable for these results. We won't just throw money at our problems—we will invest in what works. Instead of politicians doling out money behind a veil of secrecy, decisions about where we invest will be made public and informed by independent experts whenever possible.

—President Barack Obama, weekly radio address, January 24, 2009

CHAPTER 6

Borrowing Wisely

Taking his case to the American people, President Obama stumped for his stimulus plan in town hall meetings on February 9 and 10, 2009. Simultaneously, Timothy Geithner, his new Treasury secretary, unveiled the Obama strategy for resolving the credit crisis in Washington. Of the two appearances, Geithner's was more closely scrutinized across the world, in every financial market and throughout Wall Street.

Geithner was leading the charge on a bailout that would become known as "TARP II" or the second Troubled Asset Relief Program. In the first round of TARP, in October 2008, Congress pooled $700 billion to bolster banks and resolve the foreclosure crisis. Because there were few strings attached to the money, TARP ultimately amounted to a botched effort to thaw the credit freeze; hardly any of the money ended up helping homeowners, while bankers continued to pay themselves hefty salaries, bonuses, and dividends.

After about $350 billion of the $700 billion had been spent under TARP I—and rage against the banking industry was steaming like a geyser about to erupt—the Obama team decided it needed a new, more constricted approach. During Geithner's embarrassing Senate confirmation hearings (he had some issues with unpaid income taxes, which derailed two other nominees), critics were harsh with Geithner on his authorship of the previous year's mangled bailout plan, largely sponsored by Henry Paulson, the former Treasury chief under George W. Bush.

"This is a challenge more complex than any our financial system has ever faced," Geithner stated on February 10, before introducing the administration's bank-rescue program, "requiring new systems and persistent attention to solve. But the president, the Treasury, and the entire administration are committed to see it through because we know how directly the future of our economy depends on it."

The bank proposal had three basic components:

+ **Stress testing and support.** The government would examine the balance sheets of the most-imperiled banks and fund those that truly need the money. "The capital would come with conditions to help ensure that every dollar of assistance preserves or generates lending capital above the level that would have been possible in the absence of government support," Geithner said.

+ **Public-private investment fund.** Together with private investors, the Federal Reserve System, and the Federal Deposit Insurance Corporation (FDIC), this vehicle would value the worst bank loans and securities and attempt to sell them on the market at a later date. "By providing the financing the private markets cannot now provide, this will help start a process of providing a market for the real estate–related assets that are at the center of this crisis." A fund would purchase "legacy" (illiquid) loans and securities "that are trading at prices below where they would be in normally functioning markets."

+ **Fixing securitization.** This was perhaps the most ambitious piece of the proposal, which would help banks repackage debts and resell them as securities. Everything from mortgages to student loans was securitized before the credit crisis, although those markets shut down in late 2008. Some 40 percent of consumer lending is resold this way.

Along with the stimulus package, the banking proposal was the linchpin in the Obama economic recovery plan. Banks, which had frozen their lending because they were unable to sell their repackaged debts, hoarded their funds in the wake of the housing meltdown. They were afraid to lend because they were stuck with bad debts, spooked by the foreclosure spiral, and fearful of taking on more "nonperforming" loans. Without functioning credit markets, few people could get mortgages or auto or appliance loans. The government needed people to spend in order to spur the economy, but Americans could not spend if the banks wouldn't allow them to borrow.

Getting the banks working again, however, went beyond giving them more capital and trying to sell off their toxic debts. In fact, regulated bank failures were a relatively small problem. Three banks failed in 2007 and twenty-five failed in 2008, compared with more than 10,000 bank failures in 1933. The Olympian task was fixing the mortgage markets *and* banks. Geithner's overall rescue also needed to rehabilitate the badly wounded Federal Home Loan Mortgage Corporation (Freddie Mac) and Federal National Mortgage Association (Fannie Mae), which either guaranteed or securitized $5.2 trillion of the $12 trillion U.S. home-loan market. The government seized both of the quasi-public firms in the autumn of 2008, wiping out their public shareholders and placing them into a state of limbo known as *conservatorship*.

Fannie, which was set up under Franklin Delano Roosevelt's New Deal, was designed to be the safety net of the housing market. It bought loans, usually prime mortgages with creditworthy borrowers, then packaged them into debt securities and resold the bundles to investors across the world. But hobbled by homeowners who stopped paying their loans, Fannie and Freddie (established in 1970) started a downward spiral in 2008, prompting the government takeover toward the end of the year. That year, the U.S. housing market lost more than $3 trillion, with one in six homeowners owing more than the value of their homes. That stunning figure meant that the value of the 31 million mortgages and securities that the lending enterprises owned declined as well. By the end of 2008, the government pledged $200 billion to keep the giants afloat. Yet James Lockhart, the chief regulator of the companies, told Congress that if the housing market continued to deteriorate, the mortgage giants would need even more to survive.

Geithner did little to reassure the country or markets that the mortgage, housing, and banking crisis would end soon. Under TARP II, Geithner outlined a plan that could cost as much as $2 trillion. That was in addition to the $350 billion already spent on TARP I in 2008 and the nearly $800 billion stimulus program. He pledged to spend as much as $50 billion to prevent foreclosures and as much as $600 billion to buy mortgage-backed securities from Fannie and Freddie (see Chapter 7). Was this the panacea the stock and bond markets were looking for? The day it was announced, the stock market gave it a vulgar Bronx cheer as the Dow Jones Industrial Average plummeted more than 300 points. It could take years before the real answer would be known, and it would depend heavily on how it was executed and whether it truly purged the system of bad debt and eased the credit crunch.

By early May 2009, the Treasury Department and Federal Reserve provided a snapshot of what needed to be done to further rehabilitate the banks. After conducting dubious "stress tests" of the largest institutions, they found none to be insolvent, as had been earlier feared. However, the Treasury Department estimated that Bank of America Corporation, Wells Fargo & Company, and Citigroup would need approximately $75 billion in capital. Because the TARP program had $110 billion left in its kitty, the industry and markets breathed a temporary sigh of relief. By late May, there was evidence that the credit crunch was easing as interbank-lending rates were nearly back to normal.

Why the Bank Plan Needs to Work

Our society is addicted to leverage. Like the government, millions of Americans and companies borrow every single day just to stay afloat. Some borrow to stave off medical bill collectors. Others are financing a lifestyle they cannot afford, while prudent borrowers pay off their credit cards every month in what amounts to an interest-free loan.

In recent years, though, the abundance of credit has become a curse that has created an undead economy. The banks are still open (for now), the credit-card offers still come in the mail, yet there is a sense of urgency and utter dread that the economy we have borrowed to create is crumbling like an ancient, decrepit temple. The edifice of our leveraged world is falling apart, and we either need to prop it up or run the risk of becoming buried under the weight of our own debts. It is too late to tear it down and start over. Although Obama's team will have its hands full just dealing with the banking debacle, part of any comprehensive rescue will need to be restoring a reasonable amount of borrowing ability to average Americans.

Modern life is all about credit, unless you are able to pay cash for everything, a luxury few people have. You want to start a business, buy a car or a home, or cover an emergency furnace repair? For most people, easily accessed credit is their safety net. It is not a very secure one because it enables people to spend far beyond their means. Sometimes when I see Amish or Mennonite families in Chicago's Union Station en route to somewhere, I have this secret envy. Their rules of social conduct seem strict and confined to outsiders, but they are free in so many ways because they are not shackled to debt.

Credit-card debt totaled about $1 trillion for the first time in history in 2008, according to the Federal Reserve. The reasons are myriad, but the principal cause is that plastic has become the last resort to pay bills and keep lifestyles flowing. During the housing boom, the credit addiction was fed by home equity. Homeowners simply refinanced with cheap mortgage money and tapped the ballooned value of their homes, raising the amount they owed. These "cash-out re-fis" paid for boats, cars, home improvements, college tuitions, and vacations, and they often liquidated credit-card bills. Between 2001 and 2007, Americans took out $1.4 trillion in cash from their homes in refinancings and $1.2 trillion in conventional home-equity loans. These figures, compiled by the Federal Reserve, alerted the world's most powerful central bankers that Americans were leveraging at a time when home price appreciation was clearly unsustainable.

Alan Greenspan, who was chairman of the Federal Reserve from 1987 to 2006, had intimate knowledge of the equity gorging. He personally did the research and ran the numbers on home-equity debt in 2006 by coauthoring a high-profile research report for the Fed. Greenspan and other top officials knew that Americans were not only overborrowing against their nest eggs but also doing it during a bubble, one that would have a catastrophic impact in future years.

When the bubble burst, leaving those who had overleveraged in financial disarray, the credit industry pulled in its horns. All of a sudden, the lenders were risk averse and started to cut off all but the safest of borrowers.

Enter the Credit Crunch

During the credit crunch, banks suddenly decided that mortgage borrowers needed to put down 20 percent to 25 percent in cash to qualify for a loan. The subprime and "Alt-A" markets were, in effect, shut down for credit-challenged borrowers. Private mortgage insurance rose from 0.5 percent of a home's price to 0.75 percent. Banks then clamped down on home-equity loans; more than 75 percent of lenders tightened standards.

Credit-card standards were next, with more than half of banks becoming more restrictive. As a result, lines of credit were reduced, more fees were added for late payers, and millions of customers were dropped. Private student-loan rates rose by a full percentage point. Small businesses were denied loans and had to resort to borrowing on credit cards. The days of casino credit ended sometime in late 2007 and became a full-fledged credit meltdown in 2008 that extended from tire-plant workers in Akron, Ohio, to multinational banks in New York.

For those people who could count on the more easily accessed world of credit-card borrowing, it was like rushing from one burning building to the next. Although plastic debt is unsecured—you cannot lose your home if you do not pay—it has always been a profit center for banks. The reason is straightforward: most people do not pay within a monthly grace period, so they are charged interest and fees. The higher the balance, the more money the banks make. In fact, they benefit more if you *never* pay off the principal; their profits come from the finance charges. Unlike fixed-rate mortgages, where the term is set when you sign the contract, most credit-card companies can charge any fees or rates they want and raise these with little warning.

What sound like bargains to cash-strapped borrowers are onerous arrangements. In late 2008, the average annual percentage rate for a fixed-rate credit card was about 13 percent, 11.5 percent for a variable-rate card. When the global lending crisis enveloped the credit-card arena, banks freely doubled and tripled rates and accompanying fees. Compare those charges to a thirty-year fixed mortgage, which was available for about 5 percent in early 2009, and you can see how expensive plastic credit has become. The truth is, credit cards have always been among the most expensive ways to borrow, and they only became more usurious during the crunch.

Credit-Card Practices That Needed to Change

There are layers of fees that only add to the misery and total expense for those who cannot pay on time. Not only are additional fees levied *automatically* without warning, but also banks have been able to cloak them in opaque and nearly indecipherable language. Here is how the small print works against you in many of the most abusive credit-card agreements:

- **Retroactive rate increases.** Card issuers raise your rate and apply it to past purchases.
- **Changes without justification.** Banks can change any rule for any reason.
- **Universal default.** Every missed payment can be subject to a penalty, even if it was with another issuer. Nothing is forgiven.
- **Late fees galore.** Banks have been levying late fees even if your payment was mailed on time. This abuse has been poorly policed because of the lack of strong federal regulation.
- **Double-cycle billing.** This charming practice will hit you for late fees and penalties a full month after you have paid your balance.
- **Over-limit fees.** Charge more than your stated limit? Pay up with another round of penalties.
- **Deceptive offers.** Issuers trumpet a "low, low rate" that compels you to transfer your balance from another card. That rate turns out to be only for a short period of time or a variable rate. In both cases, your rate increases.

Other Shifty Practices

It is well known that payday lenders, operating under loose state regulations, have been able legally to charge borrowers as much as 4,000 percent in annual rates. These loan shops, which can be found in most lower-income communities and on the Internet, operate largely unfettered by federal regulation, although they do have to fully disclose their charges.

Even more insidious are overdraft loans through banks. Say you open a checking account and sign up for "overdraft protection." Instead of charging one flat fee per overdraft, your bank has essentially given you an expensive line of credit. Like many forms of credit, they are little understood, and charges rack up the longer you have an unpaid balance. The Consumer Federation of America estimates that Americans pay more than $17 billion in overdraft loan fees annually, so these credit lines have become additional profit centers for banks.

Overdraft fees sneak up on customers because banks may not clearly disclose how they work. For example, someone who overwithdraws money from an automated teller machine may be subject to them. Debit-card transactions also trigger them. The FDIC studied these charges in 2008 and found that banks automatically enroll customers in the most expensive overdraft options and target lower-income customers with exorbitant rates.

None of these abuses are news to Congress or the Obama administration. They have been going on for years and have been documented by the Government Accountability Office and a wide range of consumer groups led by the Consumer Federation of America and Consumers Union. Because federal regulation of the credit industry was poor to begin with and entrusted largely to weak state regulators, any policing of the business would be an improvement. Tough federal laws are needed. Even better, tougher *lawmakers* are necessary to resist the powerful banking lobby.

Fortunately, the Federal Reserve approved new rules in 2008 to rein in some of these practices (see the box on credit-card practices on the previous page). The downside: the rules do not go into effect until

2010 and lack the power of federal legislation. Other shortcomings included failure to regulate size and duration of penalty rates, phone and Internet payment fees, abrupt credit-limit reductions, deceptive offers, and oversoliciting to students.

An even more comprehensive way of addressing credit-card abuses would be to increase education to cardholders, require courses on prudent credit use in all high schools (some provide this now), and promote savings over debt. If Obama manages to make a dent in the credit culture, it will be an important first step in the healthy delever-aging of America.

Mortgage Abuses

Part of the blame for the wave of toxic debt that has crippled the world financial system rests squarely on the shoulders of federal and state regulators. Mortgage brokers and bankers clearly knew that all they had to do was close mortgage deals. Once that initial process ended, they collected their fees and sold the loan to someone else, either the mortgage giants Freddie Mac and Fannie Mae or third parties who "securitized" the loans into opaque debt packages called *collateralized debt* (or *mortgage*) *obligations*. The more loans the brokers closed, the more frontline money merchants made. Who was the watchdog? Ratings agencies blessed these packages with their highest credit evaluations, not knowing—or perhaps not *wanting* to know—that these bundles were loaded with holes. Nobody inspected the loans and securitized "tranches" for problems either when they were issued or when Wall Street gorged on them. When massive defaults did occur and thoroughly infested bank balance sheets in 2008, far too many politicians in Washington acted in horror and surprise.

When home prices were rising, nobody had any idea housing values would drop the way they did. Clearly, though, companies exploited credit-challenged homeowners in the selling of subprime mortgages, particularly in lower-income neighborhoods. Companies such as Countrywide aggressively targeted minorities, according to the Illinois attorney general's office. These rapacious peddlers knew that these borrowers were less sophisticated than "prime" customers with decent credit ratings and adequate income. They also knew that they could charge higher fees. Much higher fees. A study by the Center for Responsible Lending, a pioneering consumer group fighting abusive lending practices, found that subprime borrowers paid $5,000 more than prime customers over a five-year period for the same kind of loan, and they would pay as much as $36,000 more over a thirty-year term.

"For people with weaker credit, brokers consistently charged higher interest rates than retail lenders," the center's study concluded, citing brokers "emphasizing maximum revenues per loan for subprime borrowers."

These troublesome mortgages will do even more damage unless the Obama administration can undertake a complete overhaul of the industry, which will take years. The devastation of 2008, when $250 billion of mortgages were reset to higher rates, is just a prelude to a plague. By 2010, this amount will increase by another $700 billion. Unless the White House, Congress, and regulators find a way to modify or buy these loans, the foreclosure wave will continue.

CREATING A CREDIT-CARD RATING SYSTEM TO IMPROVE DISCLOSURE

What Was Promised: Obama pledged to establish a five-star rating system modeled on five-star systems used for other consumer products so that every consumer knows the risk involved in every credit card. Credit-card companies will have to display the rating on all application and contract materials, enabling consumers to quickly understand all of the major provisions of a credit card without having to rely exclusively on fine print in lengthy documents.

What Congress Passed: The Credit Card Accountability, Responsibility and Disclosure Act of 2009, which was signed on May 22, did not mandate a rating system, although several other pro-consumer protections were included (see below).

CREDIT-CARD BILL OF RIGHTS

What Was Promised: Obama promised to establish a credit-card bill of rights to protect consumers, which would include the following provisions: a ban on unilateral changes, applying interest rate changes only to future debt, prohibiting interest on fees, prohibiting so-called universal defaults, and requiring prompt and fair crediting of card-holder payments.

What Congress Passed: The Credit Card Accountability Act will do the following:

- **Ban retroactive rate increases.** Rate increases on existing balances due to "any time, any reason" or "universal default" are banned. Retroactive rate increases due to late payment are restricted.

- **Establish first-year protection.** Issuers may continue to offer promotional rates with new accounts or during the life of an account, but these rates must be clearly disclosed and last at least six months.

- **End late-fee traps.** Institutions will give cardholders at least twenty-one calendar days from time of statement mailing to pay balances. Late-fee traps such as weekend deadlines, due dates that change each month, and deadlines that fall in the middle of the day are prohibited.

- **Enforce fair interest calculation.** Card issuers will have to apply excess payments to the highest interest balance first.

- **End double-cycle billing.** The act ends the practice by which issuers use the balance in a previous month to calculate interest charges on the current month.

- **Require opt-in to over-limit fees.** Institutions will have to obtain a consumer's permission to process transactions that would place the account over the limit.

- **Restrain unfair subprime fees.** Fees on subprime, low-limit credit cards will be restricted.

♦ **Limit fees on gift and stored-value cards.** The act enhances disclosure on fees for gift and stored-value cards and restricts inactivity fees unless the card has been inactive for at least 12 months.

♦ **Require plain language.** Creditors will give consumers clear disclosures of account terms and activity. Model disclosures will be updated regularly to ensure that they remain clear, useful, and relevant.

♦ **Provide information about the financial consequences of decisions.** Issuers will need to display on periodic statements how long it would take to pay off the existing balance—and the total interest cost—if the consumer pays only the minimum due. Issuers will also have to display payment and total interest cost to retire the existing balance in 36 months.

♦ **Mandate public posting of credit-card contracts.** Issuers will be required to make contracts available on the Internet in a usable format.

♦ **Hold regulators accountable.** Regulators will be required to report annually to Congress on their credit-card protection enforcement and be required either to update the applicable rules or to publish findings if they deem further regulation unnecessary.

♦ **Protect college students.** The act contains new safeguards for college students and young adults, including a requirement that card issuers and universities disclose agreements with respect to the marketing or distribution of credit cards to students.

Although this was one of the most comprehensive reforms of credit-card regulation in a generation, the law won't go into effect until February 22, 2010. As a result, credit-card issuers have a "window" in which to raise fees, restrict credit, and continue the practices this law was designed to prevent. The major shortcoming of the law is that it fails to limit finance charges, which could soar before and after the new legislation takes effect. Obama's team lobbied hard for this law and achieved most of what the President promised.

CAPPING OUTLANDISH INTEREST RATES ON PAYDAY LOANS AND IMPROVE DISCLOSURE

What Was Promised: Obama promised to extend a 36 percent interest cap to all Americans and require lenders to provide clear and simplified information about loan fees, payments, and penalties during the application process.

What Congress Passed: Congress did not address this issue in the stimulus plan or the budget.

ENCOURAGING RESPONSIBLE LENDING INSTITUTIONS TO MAKE SMALL CONSUMER LOANS

What Was Promised: Obama promised to encourage banks, credit unions, and Community Development Financial Institutions to provide affordable short-term and small-dollar loans, and to drive unscrupulous lenders out of business.

What Congress Passed: Congress did not address this issue in the stimulus plan or the budget.

REFORMING BANKRUPTCY LAWS TO PROTECT FAMILIES FACING A MEDICAL CRISIS

What Was Promised: Obama promised to create an exemption in bankruptcy law for individuals who can prove they filed for bankruptcy because of medical expenses. This exemption will create a process that forgives the debt and lets the individuals get back on their feet.

What Congress Passed: Congress did not address this issue in the stimulus plan or the budget.

Who Benefits Most?

Everyone who seeks and obtains credit will eventually benefit from the new pro-consumer provisions. Those who need credit will be able to get it in a fair and honest way. Those who should not be overleveraged will at least have full disclosure of what they may be getting into and have the option to avoid future problems.

The guiding principle behind complete disclosure of terms is that it fosters rational decision making. Simple, concise information in mortgage and credit-card literature helps everyone. It will lower default rates for banks and help households avoid intractable debt and bankruptcy. Government aid for those who succumb to crushing debt will be in less demand. Students will have less of a burden when they graduate and enter their careers. Parents will have more money to spend on their families. Everyone wins. Social capitalism works.

What Needs to Be Done

Stringent disclosure and policing of the mortgage industry is key to preventing the credit abuses of the past. Here are some suggestions.

- ◆ **Ban incentives to juice up loan rates.** Mortgage brokers get a bonus from lenders if they deliver a loan at a higher rate. Called *yield-spread premiums* in the industry, these incentives clearly put brokers in the thrall of bankers. Either people offering mortgages should fully report and explain these costs before closing or they should be banned entirely.

- ◆ **Allow sufficient time for document review.** At closing time, borrowers typically have only a few minutes to review and digest as many as 100 pages of documents. They should have at least a week to be able to understand every piece of paper they have to sign.

- ◆ **Disclose all costs involved in a loan.** Borrowers should receive best- and worst-case scenarios for mortgage-rate resets. They should have a complete history of local property-tax and condo-fee increases (where applicable). All additional fees involving future ownership costs, such as utilities and maintenance fees, should also be disclosed. The real estate industry will howl at this idea, but it will prevent many defaults in the future.

- **Federally regulate brokers.** Currently, real estate brokers only have to fill out state forms, and have no fiduciary duties to their customers. But if these brokers are to represent borrowers, they must act in their interests. Real estate brokers should be registered like securities brokers, who are subject to national ethics and fiduciary regulations (meaning they can be sued for misconduct), testing, and continuing education.

- **Require multiple quotes before closing.** A mortgage broker should have to present at least three offers and at least two fixed-rate loans.

- **Ban prepayment penalties.** Thirty-five states already ban the practice of penalizing borrowers for paying off their mortgages early, but others do not. Clearly, such penalities have prevented many borrowers from refinancing, which has exacerbated the mortgage crisis.

- **Make brokers and lenders legally responsible for their loans.** Brokers and lenders should no longer be off the hook for bad lending practices, and their duties should not be finished once they sell a loan. Brokers and lenders should be held liable for foreclosures, because it means the borrower was not qualified for the initial mortgage. Much of the housing crisis was fomented because "investors" ending up owning the worst loans and few, if any, who made the mortgages in the first place felt any obligation to make prudent decisions at closing.

- **Mandate credit counseling, screening, or education before mortgages are closed.** There needs to be better screening of applications to see that only those who are truly qualified obtain the loans.

We know that in order to address our economic crisis, we must address our foreclosure crisis. I know Fort Myers had the highest foreclosure rate in the nation last year. I know entire neighborhoods are studded with foreclosure signs, and families across this city feel like they are losing their foothold in the American Dream. So we are going to do everything we can to help responsible homeowners here in Fort Myers and other hard-hit communities stay in their homes.

—President Barack Obama, Fort Myers, Florida, February 10, 2009

CHAPTER 7

Restoring Home Ownership: Keeping the Dream Alive

A rock-concert atmosphere animated the Harborside Event Center in Fort Myers as President Obama arrived to a packed auditorium. Cameras and cell phones were flashing as if he were a top country-music star. The crowd barely let him begin as he gave a short speech after an introduction by Florida governor Charlie Crist, a Republican. The president was in full campaign mode, although his demeanor was that of a parent lecturing a teenager who had gotten into trouble. The president made a special stop in the area as his stimulus plan went into contentious negotiations between the House and Senate.

Getting the lay of the land a few days before the president was to conduct a town hall meeting to sell his economic stimulus plan, I could not expunge the thought that an economic neutron bomb had fallen on southwest Florida. Large lots where construction had once started were abandoned. Entire blocks of condos and single-family homes were empty, either awaiting auctions or foreclosure sales. Most of the homes in places such as Lehigh Acres, about fifteen miles east of Fort Myers, were owned by banks. Laid out with 100,000 lots in the 1950s, the former cattle ranch looked parched and forlorn.

"The situation we face could not be more serious," Obama told the crowd. "We have inherited an economic crisis as deep and as dire as any since the Great Depression. Economists from across the spectrum have warned that if we do not act immediately, millions more jobs will disappear, and national unemployment rates will approach double digits. More people will lose their homes and their health care. And our nation will sink into a crisis that, at some point, will be much tougher to reverse."

During the middle of a performance that played like an arena act, someone handed him a slip of paper that said the Senate had approved his stimulus plan (the vote was 61 to 37). He addressed concerns about the moribund home-building industry, education, and employment and then went into the crowd to hug a woman who was in tears over a public-housing issue.

As he moved on to nearby Lehigh Acres, a group of GOP senators went before the cameras in Washington to blast the stimulus plan as it moved into conference committee to shape the final version of the legislation. Without offering an alternative, Senator Mitch McConnell (R-Kentucky) complained that some of the items in the bill should have been reserved for one of the many appropriations measures (spending bills) due later in the year. Other colleagues freely alluded to the "Europeanization of America" as if the stimulus would somehow turn the United States into Sweden or Estonia. While they didn't use the "S" word (socialism), they did everything they could to imply that this was the sinister intent of the legislation.

Back in Florida, the president was pumping hands and getting a glimpse at the desolation of the housing bust. In Lehigh Acres, he saw a sampling of the more than 4,000 foreclosed homes. He heard how prices tripled during the bubble (which peaked in 2006), then plummeted in 2007, clogging the Lee County courts with more than 30,000 foreclosures by early 2009—six times the national average. Yes, speculators and subprime lenders had ravaged southwest Florida, but what was to be done?

The Heart of the Housing Crisis

Investor Warren Buffett described the financial crisis perfectly when he called it "an economic Pearl Harbor" on the eve of President Obama's inauguration. There were few problems more vexing to the new administration than this one. The housing bubble that burst in 2006 was continuing to ravage credit, stock, and real estate markets well into the first year of the Obama administration, with no signs of letting up.

More than 3 million homeowners were facing foreclosure when Obama took office, and another 8 million were at risk. The last year of the Bush administration was wretched for the home market: foreclosures were up more than 80 percent from the end of 2007. Instead of the

Great American Dream, home ownership had become a nightmare for one in every fifty-four households. With housing prices down by 20 percent across the country, there were few buyers and a year's supply of unsold homes on the market. People stuck in unaffordable adjustable-rate mortgages were largely unable to refinance, even though thirty-year fixed-rate loans dropped below 5 percent when Obama took the oath of office. Millions are stuck and losing their homes.

Entire foreclosure "gulches" in central and southern California, Arizona, Nevada, Michigan, Ohio, and Florida remain frozen in economic purgatory. Subdivisions that sprouted like dandelions are half-finished and abandoned. Homes that had been bought and "flipped" by speculators (see my book *The Cul-de-Sac Syndrome*) were boarded up and repossessed by banks that could not sell them, even at 50 percent off. Congress meekly attempted to boost the home market through its HOPE for Homeowners Act in July 2008, although most of its programs were voluntary and did little to halt foreclosures.

What began as unbridled optimism in the American Dream—that you could get ahead simply by buying and selling a home—turned into a *bête noire*. Lenders like Countrywide and IndyMac gladly handed out mortgages to borrowers who had poor credit with few questions asked. In contrast to *prime* loans to people with strong credit, *subprime* loans allowed brokers to charge higher interest rates. These high-interest (and high-risk) mortgages were then bundled and packaged in the form of Wall Street securities with innocuous labels such as "collateralized mortgage obligations." The builders, real estate agents, mortgage brokers, and bankers all took their fees and then dumped these toxic securities on investors. A global credit market hungry for seemingly safe, high-yielding securities gorged on this poisonous debt. Ratings agencies either missed or ignored their risk. A shadow market of derivatives sellers sold bets on them, a kind of unregulated insurance wager that they would not fail. A range of buyers, from Norwegian cities to the largest banks in the United States, had a piece of them or traded their various derivatives on unregulated exchanges.

Because the mortgage securities were backed by actual home values (which no one expected to fall) and received the highest possible AAA scores from ratings agencies (by conflicted companies paid by their issuers to evaluate them), few people on Wall Street gave these securities a second thought. After all, who in recent memory had lost money selling an American home? The brief blip of home-market slumps in Boston in the 1990s and Los Angeles in the late 1980s were distant, if not forgotten, memories. Even as Federal Reserve Chairman Alan Greenspan championed driving the cost of lending down to practically zero during the 2001 recession, he gave little pause to how it would inflate a bubble in the wake of the dot-com bust.

When Congress essentially designated $50 billion of the $700 billion from the Troubled Asset Relief Program (TARP) funds for the Obama administration about a week before the inauguration, lawmakers hoped for a more effective plan of attack. Led by economic czar Lawrence Summers and Treasury Secretary Timothy Geithner, the Obama team had three short-term objectives: bolster banks, stop foreclosures, and revive lending and restore home equity.

Bolstering Banks. By the end of 2008, banks had written off some $1 trillion in bad debt, but an unknown amount of toxic securities were still on their books. The Obama administration considered creating a "bad bank," similar to the rescue agency of the savings and loan crisis of the 1980s. It also considered buying larger stakes in major players such as Bank of America and Citicorp. Many critics of the government's role called for outright seizure and nationalization of the banks.

Stopping Foreclosures. This would either involve buying the bad loans outright with taxpayer dollars or giving banks, courts, and investors the ability to "modify" the loans at lower rates.

Reviving Lending and Restoring Home Equity. These were the most troublesome goals. Banks will not lend money to people who may not be able to repay them when homes continue to fall in value. The first two items were essential for this third objective to be met.

Would the federal government eventually become the primary lender in the mortgage market as well as the sole guarantor of these loans over time? (It was, as I wrote this in April 2009.) Would taxpayers be stuck with a portfolio of worthless notes that would burden future generations with the debts of those who should not have received mortgages in the first place? Possibly. How would the Obama team stem the decline of a market that had been inflated by greed and unrealistic expectations?

"The next version of the housing and mortgage rescue program will need to be far bolder," wrote Robert Kuttner in his book, *Obama's Challenge*. "Only presidential leadership can accomplish that."

Obama's campaign platform aimed to provide direct relief to help America's homeowners pay their mortgages, stay in their homes, and avoid painful tax increases. Although Congress did not follow through on many of Obama's promises in its stimulus package, many of Obama's campaign promises were ultimately addressed in the $75 billion Homeowner Affordability and Stability Plan that Obama and Geithner unveiled on February 18, 2009. Because the plan uses many of the resources of the Housing and Economic Recovery Act (which passed July 30, 2008), Obama's team said it did not need to return to Congress for more funding.

MODIFYING MORTGAGE TERMS

What Was Promised: Obama promised to instruct the secretaries of the Treasury and Housing and Urban Development to use their authority to aggressively modify the terms of mortgages. Obama was an early champion of the HOPE for Homeowners Act that passed July 30, 2008, to prevent foreclosures. In addition, Obama insisted that Congress's financial rescue include provisions to authorize the Housing Secretary to modify the terms of mortgages for homeowners who played by the rules. Obama also called for state housing agencies to coordinate broad mortgage restructurings. Though the HOPE act gave states broader authority to help struggling homeowners, homeowners were largely unable to get the help they needed from this first residential-bailout measure.

What Congress Passed: On May 20, 2009, President Obama signed the Helping Families Save Their Homes Act, along with the Fraud Enforcement and Recovery Act. The Fraud Act doubled the FBI's budget for investigating mortgage scams to $165 million. In 2008, the Treasury Department received 62,000 reports of mortgage fraud, although the actual number is much higher. The law also made it a crime to overvalue a property to influence mortgage bankers.

The Helping Families Act bolsters provisions of the 2008 HOPE for Homeowners Act by aiding homeowners facing foreclosure. People who owe more than their homes are worth will get more help from loan servicers and lenders to stay in their homes and refinance. Rural housing and Federal Housing Administration loans will be eligible for modifications to reduce interest rates. Renters living in foreclosed homes will receive 90 days' notice of foreclosure action. Although not a foreclosure prevention measure, homeowners will be notified any time their mortgage is sold or transferred. Borrowing authority for the Federal Deposit Insurance Corporation and National Credit Union Administration was increased to better protect insured deposits.

In addition, the Obama administration put in place a new program called the Homeowner Affordability and Stability Plan in mid-February 2009. The plan features the following provisions.

Reduced Monthly Payments. The Affordability and Stability Plan promised to reduce monthly payments for as many as 9 million families. For example, if a borrower has payments adding up to as much as 43 percent of the total household income, the lender would have to bring down interest rates so that the borrower's monthly mortgage payment is no more than 38 percent of the total household income. Next, the initiative would match further reductions in interest payments—dollar for dollar with the lender—to bring the ratio down ultimately to 31 percent. The lender must keep the lower interest rate in place for five years; after this, the lender could gradually increase it to the rate that was in place at the time of the modification. For each of the five years that a borrower stays current, the plan will provide a monthly balance reduction on the mortgage payment, as much as $1,000 a year. Lenders will also be able to bring down monthly payments by reducing the principal owed on the mortgage, with the Treasury sharing the costs. Companies that handle loan payments, known as *servicers*, will receive an up-front fee of $1,000 for each eligible modification meeting the guidelines of the initiative. They will also receive "pay for success" fees of as high as $1,000 a year for each mortgage for three years, as long as the borrower stays current on the loan.

Reaching Borrowers Early. To keep lenders focused on reaching borrowers who are trying their best to stay current on their mortgages, an incentive payment of $500 will be paid to servicers, and an incentive payment of $1,500 will be paid to mortgage holders if they modify at-risk loans before the borrower falls behind.

Home Price Decline Reserve Payments. To encourage lenders to modify mortgages, the administration, together with the FDIC, developed an insurance fund that will discourage lenders from foreclosing on mortgages that could be viable out of fear that home prices will fall even further later on.

Relocation and Rehabilitation Funds. The government will provide $1.5 billion in relocation and other forms of assistance to renters displaced by foreclosure and $2 billion in neighborhood-stabilization funds to help communities buy and fix foreclosed or vacant homes. Homeowners could find out if they qualify for any help under the Stability Act through the Web site http://www.makinghomeaffordable.gov/.

REFORMING THE BANKRUPTCY CODE

What Was Promised: Obama promised to reform the bankruptcy code and remove legal impediments to encouraging mortgage restructuring. Obama called for legislation to close the loophole in the bankruptcy code that allows bankruptcy judges to modify the terms of mortgages on investment properties and vacation homes but not on primary residences. Obama also said he would work to clarify the legal liability of mortgage servicers so that those who work with struggling homeowners to modify their mortgages will receive legal protections. He also promised to remove any tax- or legal-related impediments to encouraging shared-equity mortgages within the HOPE for Homeowners process.

What Congress Passed: A measure to allow homeowners to write down mortgage principal in bankruptcy passed the House but failed to pass the Senate in early May 2009, so this key element of foreclosure relief didn't make it into law (or had not as this book went to press). This failure will likely allow thousands of foreclosures that might otherwise be stopped.

NINETY-DAY FORECLOSURE MORATORIUM

What Was Promised: Obama promised to enact a ninety-day foreclosure moratorium for at-risk homeowners who were acting in good faith. Under this rule, financial institutions involved in the bailout would have to adhere to a homeowner's code of conduct, including a ninety-day foreclosure moratorium for any homeowners living in their homes who are making good-faith efforts to pay their mortgages.

What Congress Passed: No legislation was passed to enact this, although some large lenders imposed their own temporary moratoriums before the Treasury Department's stability program described earlier. Foreclosures continued, however, after that period, and it's not known (as this goes to press) whether the administration's program has been effective.

UNIVERSAL MORTGAGE TAX CREDIT

What Congress Promised: Obama promised to enact a 10 percent refundable tax credit on the mortgage interest paid by American families who do not itemize their taxes. (Some 65 percent of filers don't take the deduction.) This credit would help offset the cost of mortgage payments for at least 10 million middle-class homeowners.

What Congress Passed: First-Time Home-Buyer Tax Credit. Even though Obama was not able to get a universal mortgage tax credit in place, Congress did approve a first-time home-buyer tax credit in the stimulus package. In a flawed move to revive home buying in July 2008, Congress created a $7,500 credit for first-time purchasers ($3,750 for married individuals filing separately). It had little effect, however, as it was tainted by the fact that you had to *pay back* the credit in equal installments over fifteen years. Who wanted to take an additional tax liability when buying a home, even though it amounted to an interest-free loan? Congress simply amended that provision in the stimulus law to remove the repayment rule. The new *$8,000* credit would only apply to homes bought after December 31, 2008, so buyers who purchased in 2008 still have to pay the credit back under the old terms. Because the new provision does nothing to repair the secondary mortgage market, it will not facilitate lending long term. Changing tax policy also did nothing to stem foreclosures, which continued unabated when this credit became law. Few investors or home buyers will buy in a market without guarantees or without knowing that the home-price decline has bottomed out. The credit phases out if you make more than $150,000 and are filing jointly; the number is $75,000 for singles.

Who Benefits Most?

First-time home buyers will benefit when they get $8,000 back, assuming that their credit records are good enough to qualify for a loan. As a result of the credit crunch, lenders tightened up their qualifications so that only the most creditworthy (clean credit records, consistent employment) could obtain mortgages. The age of the "no-documentation" or "liar" loans had largely ended by 2007.

The stability plan aims to help these core groups: (1) people who were hit by higher (unaffordable) adjustable-loan rates but could not refinance and (2) the 6 million people facing foreclosure because they lost their jobs or fell behind on their payments for other reasons. Obama made it clear that he was out to save neighborhoods ravaged by foreclosures; when a home is foreclosed, neighboring homes lose as much as 9 percent of their value. Homeowners in foreclosure or who had their homes repossessed by lenders were largely left behind by this program. The stability plan, unfortunately, will do little to help communities already ravaged by foreclosures.

The stability plan also aids families who just got hurt by the receding tide of home values, or those whose mortgage balances exceeded their home values. For example, let's say a family puts down a required 20 percent deposit of $53,000 on a $260,000 home. This family borrows the remaining $207,000 through a thirty-year fixed-rate mortgage at 6.5 percent. However, because of a 15 percent decline in market values, the home is now worth $221,000. This makes the family ineligible to refinance with most lenders because it is now, in effect, borrowing $207,000 on a $221,000 home—giving the family less than 20 percent in equity on the home. Under the stability plan, the family would be able to refinance at 5.16 percent and lower its annual payments by more than $2,300 because the lender would have leeway to modify the loan with a lower rate. That is assuming that the homeowners qualified for the new program and the lender or servicer agreed to redo the mortgage at the more affordable terms. The stability plan is voluntary, so there are no mandates to force lenders to ease mortgage terms; the total number of homeowners helped may be drastically lower than the administration's estimates. At-risk homeowners would benefit by lowering the ratio of their mortgage payments to household income. In this case, the government would work with lenders to ensure their ratios go down to 31 percent.

Another part of the stability program would allow Freddie Mac and Fannie Mae to increase the value of their mortgage holdings by $50 billion to $900 billion. The Treasury will also be purchasing as much as $200 billion of the mortgage insurers' securities. This was an indirect way of guaranteeing some of Freddie's and Fannie's debt securities. Ultimately, it was hoped, this would allow the mortgage giants to make more loans at lower rates. As this went to press, Fannie and Freddie mortgages accounted for three-quarters of new U.S. mortgages, effectively *nationalizing* most home loans after the credit crunch forced private lenders to pull back.

With the stability plan, there was a quantum leap made to guarantee or modify nearly 10 million mortgages. In itself, this was not enough to clear out nearly a year's worth of home inventory (as of June 2009), but it was an important first step in restoring confidence to the mortgage market. With government backing through Freddie Mac and Fannie Mae, lenders would likely make loans again, thus reviving housing. When mortgage rates dropped in February 2009, as officials hoped they would, it also spurred refinancing, although mostly for homeowners who had no problem paying their mortgages.

The stability plan will only target homeowners who commit to making payments to staying in their homes and, in the language of the plan, "it will not aid speculators or house flippers." If the home credit and stability plan succeeds, it may take more than a year to really show results. If so, it would mark a brighter day for bankers, mortgage brokers, real estate agents, loan servicers, home builders, and, homeowners stuck in homes that they could not sell or refinance.

What Needs to Be Done

As 2009 dawned, not only were the worst loans in default but also prime adjustable mortgages (those with the best credit ratings) were added to the list of troubled debt. More than half of American homeowners owed more on their homes than they owned.

Without meaningful government intervention, the housing market is likely headed for more declines. Few lenders are interested in properties in markets where there is no floor to asset values. Brakes are needed to stop one of the largest asset-price declines in American history.

Perhaps full guarantees of *all* mortgages under a certain value would be the first step in guaranteeing home ownership. Although it's not clear how much this would cost taxpayers (it will not be cheap), it may be essential if the Obama administration is serious in restoring faith in the American Dream. Mortgage buyers (on the secondary market) will not likely emerge in significant numbers unless mortgage guarantees remain in place, comprehensive foreclosure reform is enacted, and home prices across the board stop falling (they continued to drop in most cities as this went to press). Few people want to invest in a home in a declining market that has no bottom in sight.

Then there is the larger question of fixing the banking system. Stock investors punished banks, insurers, and other financial-service companies that carried the heaviest load of mortgage securities. As a result, the entire global banking community has become conservative, leading to a credit crunch that has nearly shut down lending from San Francisco to Frankfurt. Bank balance sheets will need to be cleaned up through government intervention, a plan to buy the toxic assets, nationalizing the banks, or shutting down the worst banks.

The next phase of Obamanomics will have to confront some major conflicts concerning home ownership. If it is still a cherished, national goal to allow as many people as possible to buy homes, then the government will have to stand behind the mortgage market and abolish the practices that led to its decline. Banks may be forced to keep loans on their books instead of securitizing them. Brokers will have to come under much more scrutiny by stronger regulators and be held liable for giving out loans to those who do not qualify. Wall Street may be pushed out of the mortgage business entirely. These are some of the least radical solutions.

Then there is the ugly scandal of how mortgages morphed from being the safest income vehicles in the world to toxic waste that nearly collapsed the world financial system (see *The Cul-de-Sac Syndrome*). As the Obama team tackles financial regulation, it will need to put in place numerous safeguards to ensure that ratings agencies honestly evaluate the worst debt security packages (maybe by changing how they are compensated), to ensure that property appraisers don't overvalue homes, and to compel mortgage brokers to investigate borrowers' finances closely.

The bottom line is that the Obama team needs a solid, comprehensive approach to the financing, regulation, and ownership of residential real estate (and related securities and derivatives), or the American Dream will be severely impaired for decades to come.

This is a cost that now causes a bankruptcy in America every thirty seconds. By the end of the year, it could cause 1.5 million Americans to lose their homes. In the last eight years, premiums have grown four times faster than wages. And in each of these years, 1 million more Americans have lost their health insurance. It is one of the major reasons why small businesses close their doors and corporations ship jobs overseas. And it's one of the largest and fastest-growing parts of our budget. Given these facts, we can no longer afford to put health-care reform on hold.

—President Barack Obama, address to Congress, February 24, 2009

CHAPTER 8

Health-Care Reform

As Barack Obama took office and had to deal immediately with the triple jolts of the credit crisis, job losses, and the foreclosure rout, he linked affordable medical coverage to overall financial security.

As one of his first official acts as president, Obama signed the Children's Health Insurance Program into law, providing health care for 11 million children. He also urged an overhaul of the inefficient public-private patchwork that splits coverage between huge public programs such as Medicare and hundreds of thousands of individual plans. His 2010 budget built on his health-care commitment, setting aside a $634 billion pool of funds for an unspecified new program. The most visible part of his health-care reform plan in the early days of his administration was digitizing health-care records. However, this plank in his campaign platform was cast as more of a job-creation stimulus and stepping-stone to broader reform than as a large-scale restructuring.

As a temporary fix, he also managed to partially subsidize some health care through the Consolidated Omnibus Budget Reconciliation Act (more commonly known as Cobra) for the unemployed (see Chapter 1) while sending funds to states to bolster Medicaid, the federal and state medical program for the indigent. But ultimately, as the pressing reality of more than 10 million unemployed took center stage, the Obama administration had to shelve much of his health-care plan in the early months of his administration. Although incremental provisions in his campaign proposals addressed making policies available to the uninsured and small business, specifics were lacking as he tackled other economic maladies in the first sixty days of his term. In the meantime, the current health-care program resembled a minefield.

A Problematic System

When it comes to health care and the U.S. economy, Federal Reserve Chairman Ben S. Bernanke described a type of economic cul-de-sac. "Improving the performance of our health-care system is without a doubt one of the most important challenges that our nation faces," stated the Fed chairman in a speech in Washington, DC, on June 16, 2008.

Other than employment and the banking and housing crisis, health care will be the most pressing personal finance issue of our time unless the system is reformed to ensure universal access, cost control, and long-term financing. To understand how pervasive the problem of medical spending is in the United States, you need to digest some numbers on how much it is eating up in terms of national output.

As of early 2009, health expenditures consumed about 16 percent of the U.S. gross domestic product. Medical insurance claims 20 percent of median family income, compared with 8 percent in 1987, according to the New America Foundation (http://www. newamerica.net), a progressive research organization in Washington. Karen Davis, president of the Commonwealth Fund, one of the most influential think tanks on the health-reform front, also sees the economic importance of the issue.

"With 116 million adults under age 65 reporting health-care–related financial issues," she stated, "the nation's health-care crisis and economic crisis have become inextricably intertwined. As unemployment grows, more Americans will join the ranks of the uninsured."

Yes, most reasonable people will argue, but don't *most* Americans still have health coverage through their employers? I'll have to qualify that answer. Although it is true that the majority of large employers (those with more than 200 employees) offered health care, slightly less than half of the smallest businesses did. Generally the smaller the business, the fewer the benefits. With the cost of health care outpacing inflation, more employers (of all sizes) are passing along the costs of coverage. Employees paid an average of $3,354 out of their own pockets for medical expenses in 2008, according to the Kaiser Family Foundation, a research organization that tracks health issues. Even those with insurance may be *underinsured*, including about 25 million people in addition to the 47 million uninsured; these people could still could face bankruptcy because of out-of-pocket expenses for charges not covered by their plans.

Because employees, and those with Medicare, are not covered for about one-quarter of total annual medical bills, they have to make decisions on what kind of care to cut back on; they simply cannot afford to pay for everything. The Commonwealth Fund reports that "two-thirds of all adults under 65 report being uninsured or under-insured, forgoing needed care, or struggling to pay medical bills or accumulated medical debt." Millions would delay needed procedures or surgeries, often skimping on needed drugs and examinations.

Although the Obama budget proposal is an encouraging first step, it will do little to stem the rising cost of medical care other than to slightly reduce the costs of medical record keeping through digitization and eliminating the errors that result from the archaic paper-based system. Medical errors, inefficiency, and inadequate care in a number of areas is why the United States is ranked last in a Commonwealth Fund survey of nineteen industrialized countries on deaths that could be prevented by accessible, affordable care.

"American health care has gone haywire," wrote Robert Samuelson in the *Washington Post*. "It provides splendid care but has glaring deficiencies. It is so costly that 15 percent of the population lacks health insurance. For the extra money, we receive no indisputably large benefit in national well being."

Samuelson was largely referring to a study conducted by the McKinsey Global Institute that showed what Americans were getting for their health-care dollars: we were spending $650 billion more on medical bills than countries with comparable wealth. That's "twice as much as we spent on food in 2006, and more than China's citizens consumed altogether." All told, McKinsey estimated that we are spending 68 percent too much on health care. Where is the money being wasted? Doctor's fees, hospital visits, emergency rooms, dental care, diagnostic imaging, and ambulatory care. Are we any healthier for the premium price we pay for treatment in the United States? All major indicators from the World Health Organization and the Commonwealth Fund suggest that we are not.

Insured and Bankrupt

Donna Smith, a Chicago-based community organizer with the California Nurses Association, went bankrupt because of medical bills when she got cancer at the same time that her husband developed a series of heart problems. She and her husband *had* insurance through her employer, but they still lost their home. After testifying before Congress and appearing in Michael Moore's film on insurance abuses, *Sicko*, Smith is fighting for a single-payer health program. Smith and millions of others say that the only way to stem the abuses of for-profit health care is to create one large system.

"Having health insurance doesn't protect us from financial ruin or even from being denied a life-saving treatment," she told me. "It is a business arrangement in which we are in a weakened and disadvantaged position."

Another pernicious woe of the current health-care system is its booming costs. Although Obama's amorphous health-care reform plan had many critics, even they were reluctant to criticize the boondoggle of the Medicare drug plan passed during the Bush years, which fails to completely cover seniors (there's a "donut hole" where coverage disappears). Most members of Congress voted for it. Worse yet, instead of the program employing its purchasing power to negotiate the best possible deals on drugs for participants, it *pays* pharmaceutical companies to offer their products.

During the Bush administration, inclusion of a flawed subsidized drug benefit and partial privatization of Medicare was turning the popular program into a financial albatross. Providers within Medicare Advantage, an expensive and largely failed attempt to introduce managed care into the program, raised their premiums 13 percent when Obama took office. That was five times the rate of 2007 premium hikes. The Advantage cost spiral was emblematic of the private system. Costs were running out of control because there were no incentives to contain them. Patients with jobs rarely saw bills, which went to their employers or third parties. Only the unemployed, under-employed, and small-business owners knew what health care really cost, and they were getting hammered.

Here are some key facts:

- Life expectancy is directly connected to medical coverage. Uninsured and underinsured Americans visit doctors less frequently and eventually pay more for care and have the highest rate of preventable deaths before age 75.
- Employers who do not offer coverage are less competitive in a global marketplace. Workers who do not have policies end up in emergency rooms, demanding costly care that taxpayers will ultimately finance. Those who are worried about health care or medical bills are not productive members of society.
- The current patchwork system is unsustainable. Unless the growing bite of health costs is addressed by 2017, health-care spending will double from 2007 levels, consuming one out of every five dollars produced in the United States, according to the government's Center for Medicaid and Medicare Services.
- Even though many people believe the United States has the best system in the world, this is not completely true. The current mélange of U.S. health coverage ranks poorly compared to other industrialized countries, even though the United States spends twice as much per capita on medical expenses, according to the Commonwealth Fund (http://www.commonwealthfund.org).

Paying for It All

Obama's initial budget blueprint essentially channels tax revenues from wealthy individuals (those making more than $250,000 annually), corporations, and investment managers into a health-care pool and combines it with anticipated systemwide savings (described later in the chapter). This will serve as a $630 billion "down payment" for a fund that would likely cost more than $1 trillion to implement. The plan included the following provisions.

- ◆ Let the Bush-era tax reductions expire after 2010. Once this happens, the top marginal rate will move back to 39.6 percent from 35 percent. The increased revenue would go toward an unspecified program.

- ◆ Reduce deductions for people who make more than $250,000 per year.

- ◆ Increase favorable rates on capital gains and dividend income to 20 percent in 2011 from 15 percent in 2008–09.

- ◆ Ensure that private investment funds pay ordinary income rates of as much as 39.6 percent on income, instead of 15 percent (implementation date unknown at time of publication).

- ◆ Eliminate special favorable accounting rules for oil and gas companies.

- ◆ Reduce unnecessary hospital readmission rates to save roughly $26 billion over ten years.

- ◆ Fund the ongoing adoption of health-information technology to reduce costs.

- ◆ Expand research comparing the efficacy of medical treatments.

- ◆ Improve rural health through a $73 million infusion.

- ◆ Invest in prevention and wellness ($1 billion set aside in the recovery act) to better treat costly chronic diseases through community-based interventions.

- ◆ Reform the physician payment system to improve quality and efficiency.

All told, this ambitious and vague cost-saving program is expected to build a $634 billion kitty by 2019. The numbers may be excessively optimistic because the entire public-private system would need to adopt these measures for the dollars to flow back to the Treasury.

Political Challenges

In addition to financing one of the largest new government programs since Medicare, Obama has many political obstacles to surmount in order to implement health-care reform.

"I suffer no illusions that this will be an easy process," Obama told Congress on February 24, 2009. "It will be hard. But I also know that nearly a century after Teddy Roosevelt first called for reform, the cost of our health care has weighed down our economy and the conscience of our nation long enough. So let there be no doubt: health-care reform cannot wait, it must not wait, and it will not wait another year."

When Obama made the remarks above, he did not have a Health and Human Services secretary to champion his plan. His top pick for health czar was Tom Daschle, whose book on health-care reform, *Critical: What We Can Do About the Health-Care Crisis,* had attracted the attention of the Obama team during the campaign. Unfortunately, Daschle—a former South Dakota senator and Democratic majority leader—had not attended to his own tax liabilities; he withdrew his nomination before he had the chance to face Senate inquiries. He owed more than $128,000 in back taxes. Considering the president had campaigned on a slogan of "change you can believe in," pushing Daschle through the Senate would have tarnished Obama's credibility. Kansas Governor Kathleen Sebelius was later approved as the health secretary, although she would come into her post with a fraction of Daschle's knowledge, congressional clout, and network.

In addition to credibility, Obama needed a reserve of political capital to tackle the $2.6 trillion health-care issue. Opponents of comprehensive reform, and they were legion, were already sharpening their knives as Obama's team worked on its strategy. One of the first salvos was the conservative rubric that Obama's plan would "Europeanize" health care—that is, a universal program would somehow lower everyone's standard of living, even though there is actually more financial security with national health programs in Europe. One of the ugliest scare tactics was this: a government-run program would tell *your* doctor how to treat you and *ration* medical treatments!

Congress had several proposals for comprehensive health-care reform when Obama took office. Unfortunately, Congress had to shelve most of these ideas during the first six months of his first year in favor of short-term economic stimuli. Congress worked on the issue throughout the year in committees with the soft objective of passing some reform plan by the end of 2009. As of early May 2009, however, Congress had not addressed any of the following campaign promises.

- ◆ **Choosing insurance.** Obama promised to build on the existing health-care system, using existing providers, doctors, and plans. Patients would be able to make health-care decisions with their doctors, instead of being blocked by insurance companies. Under the plan, if people like their existing health-care policies, then nothing would change, except that their costs would go down by as much as $2,500 per year. Those people who are without insurance would be able to choose new, affordable health-insurance options.

- ◆ **Preexisting conditions.** He promised to require insurance companies to cover preexisting conditions so all Americans, regardless of their health status or history, can get comprehensive benefits at fair and stable premiums. Along these lines, Obama also required insurance companies to cover preventive services, including cancer screenings.

- ◆ **Tax credits.** A new small-business health tax credit would help small businesses provide affordable health insurance to their employees. Obama also promised to provide additional tax credits to employees for their premiums.

- ◆ **Lowering costs for businesses.** The government would reduce health-care costs for businesses by covering a portion of the catastrophic health costs that businesses pay in return for lower premiums for employees.

- ◆ **Preventing overcharges.** Obama promised to prevent insurers from overcharging doctors for their malpractice insurance.

♦ **Making employer contributions more fair.** Obama would require large employers who offer no or little coverage to contribute a percentage of payroll toward the costs of their employees' health care.

♦ **National health insurance exchange.** The establishment of a national health insurance exchange would include a range of private-insurance options, as well as a new public plan based on the benefits available to members of Congress.

♦ **Lowering drug costs.** Obama said he would lower drug costs by allowing imports of safe medicines from other developed countries, increasing the use of generic drugs in public programs, and preventing drug companies from blocking cheaper generic medicines from entering the market.

Hospital Data

Although Congress had not passed legislation at the time this went to press on any of the campaign promises above, Congress did act on Obama's promise to require hospitals to collect and report health-care cost and quality data by approving $19 billion for digital health records. Under this legislation, Congress approved direct payments to hospitals and physicians that computerize their record systems. This was the most visible and least controversial of Obama's many health reforms.

ADDITIONAL MEASURES APPROVED BY CONGRESS

♦ **$10 billion for medical research.** The National Institutes of Health would receive this amount for biomedical research into coronary disease, cancer, and Alzheimer's and Parkinson's diseases.

♦ **$1 billion for prevention and wellness programs.** Community-based interventions would be supported to focus on preventable diseases, mammograms, vaccines, and various screening tests.

◆ **$1 billion for treatment options.** Researchers would receive additional funds to "evaluate the effectiveness of different health-care services" by determining which treatments are best in different circumstances. This measure aims to provide an opening for more federal oversight of medical costs.

Who Benefits Most?

Obama's stated goal to invest in "electronic medical records and other technologies that drive down health-care costs" will be a clear boon for companies that digitize records.

What is not immediately apparent, nor recently mentioned by Obama, is how badly the American health-care industry needs to be modernized.

About 88 percent of U.S. doctors and hospitals did not use digital record systems as of early 2009. Doctors, nurses, and other professionals still largely write notes and prescriptions with pen and paper and store records in archaic binders and file cabinets, often resulting in medical errors and wrong medications and costing hospitals $6 billion annually in additional care.

Medical errors are believed to be the fifth-leading cause of death in the United States, causing from 98,000 to 195,000 deaths annually, according to studies by the Institute of Medicine and by Health-Grades (conducted in 1999 and 2004, respectively). Many, if not most, of those deaths could have been prevented with better record keeping and monitoring of tests, procedures, and outcome. In theory, any medical research institution, consultant, or auditing firm will benefit from reductions in medical errors.

The following is a list of companies that are likely to benefit from the digitization of medical records (stock symbols in parentheses):

◆ Allscripts-Misys Healthcare Solutions, Inc. (MDRX), of Chicago

◆ Athenahealth (ATHN), Inc., of Watertown, Massachusetts

◆ Eclipsys Corporation (ECLP) of Atlanta

◆ Streamline Health Solutions (STRM) of Cincinnati

As with all of the companies mentioned in this book, it is not clear if these companies will make a profit in the future, nor is it clear if they have the products that the marketplace demands. No one company has a silver bullet; these companies are simply worth considering as the stimulus funds flow into the private sector.

What Needs to Be Done

How do you save the best of U.S. health care while providing it to everyone at a reasonable cost? Creating one new, entirely government-run public program may be untenable and politically unacceptable. The road to a solution can merge both private and public interests.

Here are some ideas that will guide reform:

- **Outsource cost controlling.** The government can hire audit firms to see where costs can be cut; it could then act like an accounts payable department, while a private firm would police billing and implement best practices.

- **Negotiate the best price.** The government could work with suppliers (or hire firms that can do this) to make sure it gets the best price. Individual employers and individuals will not need to buy drugs, services, and care on their own. A single-payer plan, not an amalgam of private insurers, is best suited to take on this function.

- **End fee-for-service.** The current payment model should be changed so that medical expenses are based on performance and outcomes, not on the number of procedures performed. Doctors and hospitals may hate this idea, yet there are far too many incentives to overtest, overoperate, and overtreat in the current system.

- **Make technology an efficient part of the entire health-care system.** Sure, Americans are great at developing new diagnostic procedures, but why are medical records still mostly in paper form? A major overhaul focusing on the efficient use of technology is in order. Doctors and other health professionals should have instant access to the most effective drugs, treatments, and procedures. This may help eliminate some of the wasteful tests and surgeries that do not produce better overall outcomes. Obama's stimulus plan and budget have seeded this process, but it will take years to fully implement.

After soliciting and then receiving thousands of comments at the Obama transition office Web site (www.change.gov) and holding community meetings throughout the country, the administration was not short on ideas. Obama had tens of thousands of suggestions and several working models for reinventing the system. One of the simplest proposals, if there is such a thing, came from the California Nurses Association (CNA), a union that represents 85,000 nurses throughout the country and which had been active in lobbying for a single-payer system. The CNA presented a "Medicare for All" reform plan to Daschle before the former South Dakota senator withdrew his nomination as the Health and Human Services secretary.

Bathed in the rhetoric of an economic stimulus, the CNA plan combined job creation with system savings. "Establishing a national single-payer style health-care reform system would provide a major stimulus for the U.S. economy by creating 2.6 million new jobs, and infusing $317 billion in new business and public revenues, with another $100 billion in wages into the U.S. economy," according to the findings of the association's study, which was released in early January 2009, a week before the inauguration. The proposal echoed the principles of House bill 676, which was originally introduced by Rep. John Conyers (D-Michigan) in 2008.

The tab for the CNA plan was not small at $63 billion, though the association pointed out that it was less than 10 percent of the cost of the financial bailout plan of 2008, "six times less than the federal bailout for Citigroup, and less than half the federal bailout for AIG." In addition, the association said expanding Medicare to cover 47 million uninsured Americans (the number of uninsured in 2006, when the CNA did its study) would amount to $44 billion.

I am a bit skeptical of their calculations, but the CNA claimed to use "an econometric model of the current face of health care— applying economic analysis to a wide array of publicly available data from Medicare, the Bureau of Labor Statistics, Bureau of Economic

Analysis, and other sources." In other words, a single-payer system would share savings throughout the economy based on a large entity's ability to save on purchasing, allocation, and economies of scale. Certainly jobs would be lost in the private-insurance industry, which devotes a large portion of its resources to back-office administration. Like many economic models, it is incomplete but casts light on the virtues of paring the inefficiency of employer-based coverage, perhaps cutting some $56 billion in waste, according to the CNA estimate. Such a program would ensure that all Americans would be covered and able to choose their own providers. As in the past, a single-payer model will face political and semantic hurdles. Most Americans dislike the idea of government getting too involved in their health care. If positioned to emphasize guaranteed care and personal choice, the CNA plan might be called "iChoice." Whatever emerges as "the" plan, it must be marketable, provide tangible benefits for everyone, and produce real savings.

Like many stimulus models, the CNA assumes a multiplier effect by channeling money into one program. The basic assumption is that every direct health-care dollar creates nearly three additional dollars in the U.S. economy. In its *current* form, our health-care program does the following:

♦ generates 45 million jobs, directly and in other industries;

♦ accounts for 10.5 percent of all U.S. jobs and 12.1 percent of all U.S. wages;

♦ totals 9.2 percent of the nation's gross national product; and

♦ contributes about 25 percent of all federal tax revenues, as federal, state, and local taxes from the health-care sector in 2006 (the latest year for which data are available) totaled $824 billion.

According to the CNA, "a single-payer system would produce the biggest increase in jobs and wages. The reason is that the broadest economic benefits directly accrue from the actual delivery and provision of health care, not the purchase of insurance."

Expanded Medicare has several other benefits, the CNA notes, such as a streamlined system with tens of billions less in private insurance administrative waste, guaranteed choice of physician and hospital, no loss of coverage when unemployed, and no denial of coverage because of age or health status. No longer would thousands of insurers be cherry-picking only the healthiest people and gouging the less healthy and chronically ill based on their health histories or mere *propensities* for illness.

One large system also can better police tests, procedures, and best practices in addition to negotiating the lowest possible prices on everything from drugs to wheelchairs. The single-payer theory also holds that a federal health oversight authority, also proposed by Daschle in his 2008 book *Critical: What We Can Do About the Health-Care Crisis*, could regulate health care the way the Federal Reserve regulates the national money supply and monetary policy. One large regulator carries a big stick to control expenses, pool the latest research, and monitor outcomes on a scientific basis. That is a radically new model for the United States, which has relied on employers, self-insured plan administration, and the private industry to decide what is best for patients—creating an antihumanistic model. It will never work effectively as long as there's a for-profit system.

Of course, the Medicare expansion plan is one of a myriad of ideas on how to reform the system. The Commonwealth Fund also launched its own plan, which incorporated an "insurance exchange" and other efficiency measures, which was similar to Obama's proposal.

Another workable proposal was being championed by White House staffer Dr. Ezekiel Emanuel, brother of White House chief of staff Rahm Emanuel and author of *Healthcare, Guaranteed*, which outlines a sensible proposal for American health-care reform.

To create this universal coverage system, Emanuel argued for eliminating employer-provided health care and its tax subsidies while phasing out Medicare, hospital subsidies, the State Children's Health Insurance Program, and Medicaid over time. One guaranteed health-care access plan would serve everyone, saving as much as $100 billion in administrative costs. You could buy additional coverage in private markets and keep your current doctors. National and regional over-sight boards similar to Federal Reserve banks would police costs and ensure "high-quality coordinated care." The plan would be financed by a dedicated value-added tax that would fund only health care. The revenues could not be rerouted to other programs.

Why We Can't Wait

Untold numbers of Americans are under house arrest because of their medical bills. Often they were bankrupted when they got sick or injured and insurers didn't want to pay their claims. Because health premiums doubled between 2000 and 2008, fewer employers now offer full coverage, resulting in higher out-of-pocket expenses and more uncovered items. Most small businesses cannot afford health care at all.

The post–World War II social compact is fracturing more by the day. Employers were never supposed to be the ones taking care of us. They were told to rein in wages during and after the war, and they received multiple tax breaks to offer fringe benefits. Now we need a new paradigm among the government, employers, and citizens; Obama will have a large role in reshaping this paradigm.

As Bernanke observed, what is done about health care now "will affect many aspects of our economy, including the pace of economic growth, wages and living standards, and government budgets, to name a few." Because his plate has been full, the Fed chief has not offered specific remedies.

Unlike economic forecasting, the health-care picture of the future is not cloudy. There will be devastating financial consequences if we don't hunker down and prepare for a much more severe fiscal storm. Americans may be well served by an open-minded approach in creating a hybrid system that combines the best attributes of private and public health care.

Failure to rein in health costs and make care affordable and universal will be an albatross on the American economy. Employers cannot effectively compete against foreign companies that do not directly pay for health care. Either health care becomes part of the social contract or it continues to stifle American families and industry and shackle employees to companies that have coverage.

Without any change, some 61 million citizens will become uninsured by 2020—this in addition to the 25 million *underinsured* now. When that happens, health care will cost the country $42 trillion because medical costs are rising at more than 6 percent annually. That is a number you can believe in, and it can devour the nation's prosperity unless we find a way to contain it.

To preserve our long-term fiscal health, we must also address the growing costs in Medicare and Social Security. Comprehensive health-care reform is the best way to strengthen Medicare for years to come. And we must also begin a conversation on how to do the same for Social Security while creating tax-free universal savings accounts for all Americans.

—President Barack Obama, address to Congress, February 24, 2009

CHAPTER 9

Unfinished Business: Long-Range Goals in Entitlement Reform

President Obama's stimulus plan, which passed Congress in February 2009 (without a single Republican vote in the House and only three GOP votes in the Senate), will be the first major test of whether Obamanomics will have a widespread impact in healing the economy, helping the unemployed and poor, and remaking the culture in a greener mold for the future.

Before he embarked on the more ambitious journeys in his agenda, though, Obama needed to convince critics that his bailout proposals and stimulus plan were worth more than $1 trillion in taxpayer dollars. Because the legislation totaled more than 1,000 pages, many lawmakers complained they did not have enough time to read and review the stimulus bill and that it was full of pork and would burden generations with even more government debts. They were mostly right, but their objections spoke more of a political gambit than genuine concern over the country's fiscal solvency. Republicans knew that if the plan did not produce tangible signs of economic repair, then they would have the upper hand in the 2010 midterm elections because the majority of them did not sign off on the massive government program.

Because Obama has chosen to tackle some of the most divisive issues of the past thirty years, he may gain scant support in the future from conservative Republicans and Democrats on many issues. Opening his fiscal responsibility summit on February 23, 2009, he proclaimed he intended to cut the federal budget deficit in half during his term. Like many of Obama's initiatives, the claim lacks details and was largely designed to draw discussion. His team was testing the waters to see how he could approach the subject of cutting line items from his soon-to-be announced budget in a time in which the stock, housing, and credit markets were still sinking and with no bottom in sight.

Financing entitlement programs such as Medicare, Medicaid, and Social Security, which all need funding overhauls, is one of the most Herculean tasks before the Obama administration. None of Obama's immediate predecessors successfully addressed how to rein in the costs of the programs in tandem with providing adequate, sustainable funding for them for the coming generations. There is no common ground on how to restore the programs to fiscal solvency. Conservatives want to carve up Social Security and offer private accounts; liberals talk about expanding the retirement system. Obama added an element that has been percolating in congressional committees for years: an additional "universal" savings account that would replace or augment defined-contribution plans—that is, 401(k)-type plans.

Nearly everyone in Washington, though, has reached a consensus that the rate of increase in costs for the entitlement programs is unsustainable and will overwhelm government spending in coming decades. "If excess growth in health care can be brought under control," wrote Paul Krugman, the Nobel Prize–winning economist and *New York Times* columnist, in a blog from February 2009, "the entitlement problem is manageable. If not, even savage cuts in Social Security will make little difference."

Undeterred by the Republican snub on his stimulus package and softening his rhetoric about bipartisanship, Obama pressed on with his agenda, noting the need to return to a responsible budget in his weekly address from February 14, 2009.

"Our debt has doubled over the past eight years, and we've inherited a trillion-dollar deficit—which we must add to in the short term in order to jumpstart our sick economy. But our long-term economic growth demands that we tame our burgeoning federal deficit, that we invest in the things we need, and dispense with the things we don't. This is a challenging agenda but one we can and will achieve."

An Ambitious Agenda

One of the most courageous thrusts of Obama's agenda is his stated willingness to take on entitlement reform, the so-called third rail of

American politics that every president since Ronald Reagan has been unable to solve. Social Security and Medicare are now the two largest spiders in the country's social safety net. Both programs remain extremely popular but will eventually run out of money over time.

MEDICARE

"Social Security, we can solve," President-Elect Obama told the editorial board of the *Washington Post* four days before his inauguration. "The big problem is Medicare, which is unsustainable. . . . We can't solve Medicare in isolation from the broader problems of the health-care system."

To their many conservative critics, Social Security and Medicare are boondoggles. During the Bush years, various conservative think tanks devoted thousands of hours of study, special events, white papers, and full-force lobbying in their various efforts to privatize the programs. With Medicare, the free marketers won partial battles and managed to inject privately managed care and prescription-drug programs into the medical and hospital insurance system. Both of these highly subsidized provisions added to Medicare's continuing fiscal sickness by raising the overall cost of the programs.

SOCIAL SECURITY

Despite George W. Bush's jawboning, the quest to splinter Social Security into private accounts such as 401(k)s failed when Democrats manned the ramparts and vigorously defended the public system. The truth is, the Republican approach of channeling the money into private funds would have been a massive diversion of payroll funds that would do nothing to ensure more retirement security. Employees were already being fleeced in 401(k) accounts that were carved up by several layers of middleman fees. To take away the one guaranteed benefit—which was, in Franklin D. Roosevelt's words, "something that no politician could take away"—was exposed as a theft in the making. There is no realistic way the private sector can duplicate all that Social Security offers—inflation-adjusted retirement payments, death and survivorship benefits, and disability insurance—in an efficient, cost-effective way.

The privatizers who pushed to dismember Social Security in the Bush years paid little attention to the colossal inefficiencies of the 401(k) system, in which hundreds of thousands of employers have to contract for their own plans, paying additional fees for fund management, brokers, and transfer agents. Unfortunately, the current system has to change. Social Security is a numbers game that looks worse the more you run projections into the future. Though it is adequately funded for the time being, its trust fund will be exhausted by 2037 based on conservative forecasts and current trends, as laid out in the program's trustee report in 2009. When that happens, the government will continue to pay checks but only 78 cents for every dollar of benefits owed. A larger problem is an actuarial one. The baby boomers, who are 77 million strong, are one of the largest generations in American history; once they retire, there simply will not be enough workers to replace them to keep money flowing into the system's trust fund. Again, that's if nothing is done.

BUT MEDICARE IS MUCH WORSE

Social Security is not an immediate problem, so the Obama team will likely shelve it until it deals with something more pressing: Medicare. The medical program is already paying out more in benefits than it takes in from revenue sources and is projected to run out of money in 2017. In 2009, for the third straight year, trustees gave Congress a "Medicare funding warning" because more than 45 percent of the program's income is coming directly from Congress. That's a big, fiscal iceberg. How Obama's administration responds to the funding shortfall might be a prologue to how it deals with entitlement reform in general.

Similar to his "program integrity efforts" in Social Security, Obama's budget blueprint pledged to cut Medicare overpayments to private insurers (in the Medicare Advantage program), reduce drug prices, and "identify excessive payments and new processes for identifying and correcting problems."

The Medicare fix will ultimately depend on how Obama's team plans to address health-care reform in general. If a new national system is created, will it be based on Medicare, currently an unsustainable model? What if the uninsured were allowed to buy into Medicare? Would that create even more funding problems? What about a Medicare "buy-in" that would be the "public option" of a public-private system?

Fixing Social Security: The Official View

The trustees of Social Security, who issue a detailed report on the health of the retirement program and Medicare every year, have been quite frank about what could be done. Every year they lay out their "if nothing is done" scenarios and alternative approaches that make politicians' spines tingle. Their painful remedy comes down to two basic changes that can solve the problem of keeping enough money in the system to pay full benefits over the next 75 years:

- a nearly two-percentage-point increase in payroll taxes (from 12.4 percent to 14.1 percent);
- an immediate cut in Social Security payments of 13.3 percent; or
- a combination of both changes or $5.3 trillion in additional funding from Congress (that's over the next 75 years).

Obama's budget document provides unstinting support for the program and calls for allocating nearly $12 billion for administrative support and the slyly worded "program integrity efforts to ensure payments are made to the right person and in the correct amount." That was a veiled reference to cracking down on abuses in the disability-income program.

"The president is committed to ensuring that Social Security is solvent and viable for the American people, now and in the future," the budget document stated. "He is strongly opposed to privatizing Social Security and looks forward to working in a bipartisan way to preserve it for future generations." However, despite this language, there were no specific recommendations in the 2010 budget to back up this pledge.

There are several other obstacles to consider as Congress studies how to make Medicare solvent and sustainable. People are living longer and many are likely to work in retirement. They may also face a host of higher taxes for other social services, not to mention interest on the federal debt (remember that banking bailout problem?). An increased payroll tax may be inescapable.

Perhaps a national sales, carbon, or consumption tax will surface to replace payroll taxes as a source of revenue for the twin giants. Even requiring beneficiaries to pay higher deductibles needs to be on the table. No matter what consensus is reached, some sacrifices will be demanded, and it will not be an easy matter to sell them to the electorate during a recession.

LONG-TERM CARE LOOMS

Even if Obama succeeds in bolstering Social Security and Medicare, there is another aging issue looming that neither system covers with any depth: long-term care. Approximately two-thirds of Americans who turn 65 will need some form of long-term care, ranging from skilled but expensive nursing homes to in-home assistance.

A decent private room in a nursing home can cost more than $75,000 a year. Medicare generally does not cover what is known as "custodial" care, which is what most nursing homes provide. Medicare only pays for about 20 percent of all long-term care; even then, the program only pays for "skilled" care that requires the daily supervision of medical professionals.

More or less half of extended care is financed through the Medicaid system, which was originally designed to provide *only* medical care for the poor. Through an upside-down way in which elderly care is doled out, millions of middle-class families must and do impoverish themselves before they can get Medicaid to pick up the nursing-home tab because they cannot afford it on their own. Outside of Medicaid, there is no federal program that is set up to handle the more than 10 million Americans who are receiving long-term care services. Less than 10 percent of the total costs of long-term care in the United States are covered by private insurance, which is exorbitant for those 65 and older.

More than half of long-term care is a direct family matter: Children ultimately take care of their parents. These volunteer caregivers generally have neither the training nor ample time to properly care for parents. In addition, they are often stressed and inadequately supported by local services. They need help themselves, through respite care. As a result, even though the government spends $200 billion a year through its fragmented array of long-term care services, the disabled elderly often do not get the care they need. There are a few meaningful tax breaks to buy insurance, but the forecast for direct government assistance is dim as Medicaid programs struggle for adequate funding in nearly every state.

Should the Obama administration decide to enhance long-term care coverage (it has made no specific initiatives), it will provide the added benefit of relieving the burden on the Medicaid and Medicare system. Like health care in general, a basic goal would be to make long-term care insurance more accessible and affordable.

"To make private insurance more affordable, and reduce the need for underwriting (pricing policies out of reach for most people), the number of those insured must be greatly expanded. In addition, the nature of assistance for the poor must shift from the welfare-type Medicaid model to an insurance model," according to Howard Gleckman, who has studied long-term care issues for the Boston-based Center for Retirement Research.

Long-term care shares the economic inefficiency ailment of the health-care and retirement systems. One large pool, at least in terms of the law of large numbers and economies of scale, makes much more sense than splintered approaches of three or four different parties trying to pay for the same thing. The more people you have paying into the pool (or system) or buying services and products, the lower the overall costs. It works for Wal-Mart and the federal government. Why can't one big provider of health services work for the entire U.S. population?

It would not be far-fetched to imagine that part of the Obama revolution, should it reconsider elderly issues, is that the government will not need to be the provider of all of these services but will act as one big, accountable purchasing agent. It makes more sense than expecting the private sector or a messy, ineffective network of government programs to deliver what is needed.

Real Income

Retirement has a high cost for a few reasons. First, as retirees age, they have less money to pay for essential services because they are typically living on a fixed income. Second, inflation drives up costs and reduces purchasing power over time. Third, the retirement income of retirees is pinched by taxes.

The ownership society of the post-Reagan era has created another little-known unintended consequence: retirees will have lower after-tax income because of the nature of the defined-contribution system. Income from 401(k)s, 403(b)s, 457s, SIMPLEs, annuities, and individual retirement accounts (IRAs) are all subject to *taxable* withdrawals, thus reducing real income. After Uncle Sam and most states take their cuts (the notable exceptions being Alaska, Florida, New Hampshire, Tennessee, Texas, Washington, and Wyoming), inflation begins to take its toll. Few, if any, defined-contribution plans are set up to offer inflation-adjusted, annuitized payments. The only guarantees are that the *after-tax* real income will be much smaller than you think. The reason is simple: unlike Social Security, you take money out of a 401(k)-type plan through a lump sum. Unless the money is deposited into an inflation-indexed annuity (not a component of the current system), the funds will not keep up with inflation.

The fact that retirement kitties evaporated amid the country's most pernicious downturn in two generations provided Obama with political capital to address the long-term personal financial security of the middle class. Most Americans felt the hammer come down on their real, after-tax incomes at the beginning of the twenty-first century. Median income (subtracting inflation) for households headed by those under 65 dropped by $1,951 between 2000 and 2007, with the number of those living in poverty rising by almost 6 million, as was noted in the budget blueprint. "The American Dream has slowly slipped beyond the grasp of millions," the proposal states. Any comprehensive approach to bolstering retirement will have to address the need to save and beat inflation while building a retirement kitty. That was a daunting and largely unaddressed premise when Obama took office, and it will occupy Congress during Obama's term.

Unless the effect of taxes on retirement funds is addressed, millions of baby boomers and subsequent generations will find that they will not have adequate retirement income. One fire exit, at least when it comes to boosting after-tax retirement income, will open up in 2010 when IRA holders will be allowed to convert conventional IRAs to Roth IRAs, which provide tax-free incomes. Congress could also expand Roth 401(k)s; these are company retirement plans that tax contributions but not withdrawals.

Although much of Obama's political rhetoric has focused on repairing and improving the social safety net, he cannot accomplish this goal without finding methods of funding politically popular programs over the long term. It may come down to considering an entirely new way of providing money for social programs, one that will relieve the burden on Congress to revisit this dilemma every year.

Most of the hard work and political reframing that emerges from Obama's retirement security package will need to be transacted within a new budgetary framework. Not taxing retirement benefits will create a revenue hole, as will any new benefits such as an automatic retirement plan.

Obama made several proposals to reform Social Security and pension laws. Unfortunately, Congress sidelined these proposals to focus on the economic crisis. As this book went to press, Congress had not passed legislation on any of the following campaign promises.

What Was Promised

FIXING SOCIAL SECURITY

Obama promised to protect Social Security benefits for current and future beneficiaries without raising the retirement age. He also emphasized his strong opposition to privatizing Social Security. As part of his plan, the full payroll tax would remain capped at 12.4 percent, but those who make more than $250,000 a year (along with their employers) will have to pay about 2 percent to 4 percent more in total taxes.

REFORMING CORPORATE BANKRUPTCY LAWS

Reform of corporate bankruptcy laws, to protect workers and retirees, would include the following provisions: (1) Companies would have to better protect employee pensions; (2) Bankruptcy courts would not be able to demand more from workers than from executives; (3) Companies would not be allowed to issue executive bonuses while cutting worker pensions; (4) Workers would be able to increase the amount of unpaid wages and benefits they can claim in court; and (5) Companies would have to limit the circumstances under which retiree benefits can be reduced.

FULL DISCLOSURE OF COMPANY PENSION INVESTMENTS

All employees who have company pensions would receive detailed annual disclosures about how their pension funds are invested.

ELIMINATING INCOME TAXES FOR SENIORS WHO MAKE LESS THAN $50,000

Obama said he would eliminate all income taxes on seniors who make less than $50,000 per year. This would provide an immediate tax cut, averaging $1,400, to 7 million seniors; it will also relieve millions of seniors from the burden of filing tax returns.

AUTOMATIC WORKPLACE PENSIONS

A new retirement security plan would automatically enroll workers in a workplace pension plan. Employers who do not currently offer a retirement plan would be required to enroll their employees in a direct-deposit IRA account that is compatible with existing direct-deposit payroll systems. Employees may opt out if they choose. Experts estimate that this program would increase the savings participation rate for low- and middle-income workers from its current 15 percent level to around 80 percent.

EXPANDING RETIREMENT SAVINGS INCENTIVES FOR WORKING FAMILIES

In order to ensure that savings incentives are fair to all workers Obama promised to create a generous savings match for low- and middle-income Americans. The plan would match 50 percent of the first $1,000 of savings for families that earn less than $75,000, which would be automatically deposited into designated personal accounts. More than 80 percent of these savings incentives would go to new savers.

PREVENTING AGE DISCRIMINATION

Obama pledged to fight job discrimination for aging employees by strengthening the Age Discrimination in Employment Act and empowering the Equal Employment Opportunity Commission to prevent all forms of discrimination.

What Needs to Be Done

It is unlikely that the Obama administration will raise payroll taxes or cut benefits to tackle Social Security while the country is still in a recession; instead, it will need to explore more creative solutions. One option is immigration reform, which would bring millions of more workers into the system. A second option is to diversify the assets of the trust fund, which are currently nonmarketable Treasury securities, to achieve a better return. The trust fund now contains IOUs that are guaranteed by Congress, which spends the cash collected from payroll taxes. The trust fund could be run in a fashion similar to the best institutional or pension funds with diversified portfolios but geared toward stability and the income needs of future retirees.

In addition, the government needs to create flexible accounts that are not only tax free on withdrawal—most 401(k)s and all annuity proceeds are not—but guaranteed to index the rate of inflation. Only a handful of privately offered products do that today, and none of these products are government guaranteed, except for I bonds and Treasury inflation-protected securities, both of which were not designed for retirement. If this means dumping the 401(k) and its many cousins, then that is a distinct option. Should Congress decide to save these defined-contribution plans, it will need to build in numerous safeguards and guarantee an inflation-indexed annuity stream. Obama has mentioned the need for universal retirement accounts, but he did not describe how he could integrate this idea with entitlement reform.

Before a new savings revolution can begin, though, economists and political advisers need to get over the myth that savers will *not* boost the economy. People with cash cushions confidently spend on homes, businesses, college educations, vacations, and retirement. It is money they earmarked years ago.

While they are saving, the thrift-savvy are adding reserves to financial institutions, which have more money to lend and more capital to invest in businesses and new jobs. And for some reason, savers are not the least bit worried about their latest brokerage account statements, if they have them at all.

Universal retirement plans can be funded through mandatory contributions (a popular funding mechanism outside of the United States) and a firm partnership between employers on one side and government and workers on the other. Employers do not need to control these programs; government can use its big stick to negotiate the best prices for services and products while requiring financial education.

The same concept can be applied to health care. Medicare can provide prescription-drug coverage, but it should be the one purchaser who asks for the biggest discounts from drug companies. Perhaps even a consolidation of Medicare, the Veterans Administration, and the federal government's health programs would achieve even more economies of scale.

MEDICAID REMEDIES

It is clear that funding for long-term care needs to be separated from the Medicaid program, which was never meant to be the safety net for this societal need. Howard Gleckman, who has studied long-term care issues for the Center for Retirement Research, has outlined some hybrid solutions that could create a public-private partnership.

Medi-LTC. Similar to Medicare supplemental insurance or so-called Medigap coverage, these simplified insurance policies would be partially subsidized by the Medicare program but underwritten by private insurers. You would have a choice of benefit levels, depending on the amount of the premium.

Replacing Medicaid with a New Medicare-Like System. As proposed by the Urban Institute, you would obtain coverage for home and nursing-home care but be subject to a $500 annual deductible and copayment for as much as $5,000 annually. It could be funded through a payroll or value-added tax, which is similar to a German program.

Quasi-Government Plan. You would obtain a policy through a government-supervised private insurer. Enrollment would be automatic, although you could opt out, according to an earlier proposal by Senator Ted Kennedy (D-Massachusetts).

The Obama administration can best see the enormous issues of Social Security, Medicare, long-term care, and retirement reform through the lens of social capitalism. How do they partner with the private sector to deliver what everyone needs while keeping costs under control?

On a societal level, any gains in the retirement safety net would be a bold new shift into New Deal territory and an upgrading of the social contract. It may mark a transformation into what social scientist Riane Eisler calls "caring economics." This change would be characterized by a focus on caregiving, partnership, and even economic indicators that measure the value of these human services, which include child care.

"In old economic models, caring is considered irrelevant to a well functioning economy, or even an obstacle to economic success," Eisler writes in *The Real Wealth of Nations*. "In reality, the opposite is true."

More important, a stable and comprehensive safety net makes even greater innovation, entrepreneurship, and job creation possible. Americans leaving the leaky corporate umbrella will not have to worry about exclusively providing their own retirement and health care. They will be free to start up companies that make better batteries, provide toxic-cleanup solutions, or services for the disabled. The safety net could be a boon to an economy that, until the housing bust, thrived on its citizens' flexibility, mobility, and willingness to take risks.

Whether Obamanomics can seed this renaissance is not a matter of how bold the president's vision is. Although it is plenty audacious, it comes down to how much Americans rally behind it, whether it's sustainably funded over the long term, and whether Congress listens to the electorate instead of the lobbies that still have undue influence on the people's business.

The question we ask today is not whether our government is too big or too small, but whether it works—whether it helps families find jobs at a decent wage, care they can afford, a retirement that is dignified. Where the answer is yes, we intend to move forward. Where the answer is no, programs will end. And those of us who manage the public's dollars will be held to account—to spend wisely, reform bad habits, and do our business in the light of day—because only then can we restore the vital trust between a people and their government.

—President Barack Obama, Inaugural Address, January 20, 2009

CHAPTER 10

The Road Ahead

Two days after his inspiring first address to Congress on February 24, 2009, the president catapulted into the budget battle with a nearly $4 trillion agenda that advanced his call for clean energy, better education, and health care. Wielding the swords of both a fiscal cost cutter and social capitalist, he laid out his blueprint for change by proposing to raise taxes on the wealthiest 2 percent of Americans; corporations; and private investment funds. What was always called *wealth redistribution* morphed into an array of programs with tangible social and environmental benefits. It was a eulogy for the Reagan-Bush era of trickle-down economics, a formula that seemed innocuous in good times and an abject failure in 2008 and 2009, during the worst market-induced recession since the 1930s. If Obama's programs survive the congressional gauntlet, they will reignite the progressive manifesto and champion bottom-up economics for the middle class and poor.

"Just as a family has to make hard choices about where to spend and where to save, so do we, as a government," Obama said while highlighting the main points of his proposed budget. "There are times where you can afford to redecorate your house and there are times where you need to focus on rebuilding its foundation. Today, we have to focus on foundations."

By reaping revenue from the richest segments of society, Obama is striving to provide universal health care, although in the early going he never said "single-payer," "nationalized," or even "universal model." He also hopes to channel $15 billion over the next decade into clean-energy and clean-vehicle technologies, partially through revenues from carbon cap-and-trade credits. Where would the rest of the money come from? He wasn't shy in telling Americans—and Congress, his main target audience—that he wasn't going to spare the special-interest politics that has guided the porkish obesity of the budget process in the past.

> No part of my budget will be free from scrutiny or untouched by reform. We will end no-bid contracts that have wasted billions in Iraq and end tax breaks for corporations that ship jobs overseas. And we will save billions of dollars by rolling back tax cuts for the wealthiest Americans while giving a middle-class tax cut to 95 percent of hard-working families. But we will also have to do something more—we will, each and every one of us, have to compromise on certain things we care about, but which we simply cannot afford right now. That is a sacrifice we are going to have to make.

Staying true to his campaign mantra of trying to protect and bolster the middle class, Obama knew he was stirring the angry battalions of lobbyists for the health-care, pharmaceutical, petroleum, investment management, and defense industries. Whether he could employ his political capital to fend off that assault would be a key test of his agenda to remake America. In his $3.5 trillion 2010 budget, Obama managed to disturb nearly every big-money lobby in targeting the elimination of 121 programs, including items such as:

- cracking down on offshore corporate tax loopholes, which could reclaim some $190 billion for the Treasury through 2019;
- reining in more than $400 billion in federal contracting, which had doubled from 2000 to 2006;
- stepping up tax collection and reforming the tax code to collect some $300 billion from the "tax gap" caused by unpaid taxes from individuals and corporations;
- striking $50 billion in overpayments;
- cutting $26 billion in oil and gas tax breaks (savings through 2019);

◆ stopping $200 million in payments to clean up abandoned coal mines;

◆ saving $4 billion in estimated waste from Iraq-related spending;

◆ scrapping $20 million to modernize Agriculture Department programs; and

◆ eliminating more than $10 million in ineffective Education Department programs.

Keeping with his campaign and administrative mantra of transparency and accountability, Obama's budget featured myriad initiatives to police fraud and excessive spending in nearly every department. He would need to cut every possible wasted dollar because he was facing an unprecedented $1.8 trillion deficit in the 2010 budget. It was more than a daunting challenge given that during the Bush years, government outlays grew at a 3.6 percent annual rate and turned a $236 billion budget surplus at the end of Clinton's administration into a $1 trillion–plus deficit, mostly because of the Iraq and Afghanistan wars, tax cuts, and bank bailouts. Adding salt to the wounds of the crippled economy was the fact that more jobs were lost in 2008 than in any year since the Bureau of Labor Statistics began keeping records in 1939. So there was little irony in the title of the budget's introductory summary: "Inheriting a Legacy of Misplaced Priorities." It was the bitter political rhetoric of a spending plan designed to mend nearly a decade of government mismanagement.

The Big Test

Mostly divided along party lines (twenty Democrats in the House voted no), both houses of Congress passed budget resolutions on April 2. Although the Republicans would later offer their own "shadow budget" proposal several weeks later, it was filled with more tax cuts for the wealthy and basically negated Obama's stimulus spending. It was a misplaced alternative in the most trying economic climate since the 1930s. The resolutions, it should be noted, were just tacit agreements to the outlines of Obama's budget. The devil would be in the details in the coming months.

The gauge of whether Obama's economic policies succeed lies in whether his programs manage to extend the hope, promise, and stability of prosperity. It's unlikely that his administration will be able to quickly solve the vexing problems of banking solvency, foreclosures, health-care reform, or unemployment in the first year of his term. If, at the very least, his team manages to stem the economic despair from Appalachia to the Central Valley of California, it will have accomplished much.

What had gained currency during the campaign and first weeks of the Obama administration was that the economy could be salvaged, recycled, and rebuilt from the ruins of the banking and housing collapse. A new philosophy, which some progressives called the "New Economy," guided many of Obama's policies. Not to be confused with the new economy of the dot-com era—in which the Internet and communications revolutions would somehow transform every corner of the economy into independent pockets of productivity— this reawakening focused on humanistic values.

David Korten, whose work on establishing progressive, locally based, human-scale economies has resounded globally, asserts that the unfinished business of Obamanomics is to "redirect the focus of economic policy from growing *phantom* wealth to growing real wealth." That's a direct attack on the culture of Wall Street speculation, unregulated hedge funds, and the unfettered "shadow" banking system that managed to operate free of government oversight. Korten would attempt to "recover Wall Street's unearned profits and assess fees and fines to make Wall Street theft and gambling unprofitable."

What Korten is suggesting is putting a huge leash on the free market system. He would restrict corporate charters, restructure financial services (by lowering fees to consumers), and "implement policies that create a strong bias in favor of human-scale businesses owned by local stakeholders." To Korten, the financial debacle of recent years was the result of Wall Street's unfettered growth and catastrophic borrowing to achieve outlandish profits while producing nothing except huge wealth for a select few. As Korten states in his *Agenda for a New Economy,*

In 1950, arguably the peak of U.S. global power, manufacturing accounted for 29.3 percent of the U.S. gross domestic product and financial services for 10.9 percent. By 2005, manufacturing accounted for only 12 percent of the GDP, and financial services for 20.4 percent. . . . Even more than making our living selling ourselves goods made in China, we have made our livings selling pieces of paper—correction: trading numbers encoded in computer files.

Shifting Priorities

The financial crisis may provide Obama's defining moment. He was charged to set the economy right by extinguishing the bank melt-down. His 70 percent approval ratings when he took on the chal-lenge indicated that he had broad backing. Failure would mean that, unless the electorate was extraordinarily patient, his political capital would be half exhausted by the time midterm elections came around in 2010. He had to find the brakes on a runaway freight train and find a way to reverse course.

The ghosts of Franklin Roosevelt and his cousin Teddy probably paid him a visit in the early days of his presidency. What did the spir-its of Progressive reform tell him? Stick to the script. Go after the banking crisis as aggressively as possible to cut it off at the knees, but all the while focus on the long-term goals of infrastructure spend-ing, fairer economic structure, and health-care reform. Given all of the economic chips on his shoulder, will Obama be able to triumph in winning *most* of his progressive reforms? The Progressive move-ment came into being in the late nineteenth century as a bulwark against trusts and corporate control of the economy and workplace. Clean food, fair labor laws, and antitrust laws emerged from this powerful social movement. Leaders such as Robert ("Fighting Bob") LaFollette of Wisconsin moved the Progressive movement into every form of government, pushing for accountability and reform on every level (you can still see the Progressive legacy in the Wisconsin legislature).

Originally, Progressivism was a backlash to the business-dominated policies of McKinley Republicans, who were against regulation and believed that corporations knew what was best for the country. When Teddy Roosevelt became president after McKinley's assassination in 1901, he brought the Progressive agenda to the White House, press-ing for reforms in corporate regulation and environmental protection.

The New Economy Agenda

What would humanistic economics and social capitalism look like and how would they remake America? Here are some talking points:

- **People come first, not markets.** This concept would entail a strong social safety net for health care, retirement, and education. The government would take a leading role in all of these institutions.
- **Corporate democracy is key.** If we're going to have an ownership society, then shareholders will need to have veto power over out-of-control executives and bankers. They should gain more power to boot errant CEOs and directors through the proxy system and have more representation on corporate boards of directors. The corporate charter would be limited in power under this movement.
- **Phantom wealth should be taxed.** In David Korten's view, locally produced wealth is more essential to the economy than paper profits produced by Wall Street bankers and hedge funds. Speculation leads to bubbles and should be taxed in some way to prevent the devastation of market busts.
- **A pluralistic partnership should displace patrimony and corporatocracy.** Obama has already seeded this with his cybernetwork campaign, transparency, and feedback initiatives. Democracy will not thrive until all corners of society have some say in the shaping of laws and policy.

Many of Roosevelt's most ardent corporate reforms were then carried out by his successor, William Howard Taft.

The durability of Obama's progressive agenda will largely depend on the severity of the recession, congressional support, and Obama's ability to stay on course and solve the banking and housing crises. If Obama continues to enjoy a popular mandate and can move his reforms through the supply-side gauntlet on Capitol Hill, then he may be able to reverse some Bush-era policies. In that light, Obama will need to reexamine and redirect Bush's "War on Terror," which dominated the forty-third president's policy making, while Wall Street and housing speculators ran amok.

The U.S. government spends about $162 billion annually on the terror threat; that is more or less equivalent to a quarter of the first wave of the massive financial bailout program. Some 1,900 people are killed internationally by terrorist acts every year, the vast majority of those occurring outside the United States. (Approximately *seventy* U.S. citizens die every year from terrorism, according to the National Counter Terrorism Center.) Almost half a million people die from heart disease annually, although the government only spends $3 billion on related research. So, even though 6,600 times as many Americans succumb to heart disease than terrorism annually, the government spends 54 times more money to save some 70 people. Obama promised to "withdraw all combat troops in Iraq by 2010," although it wasn't clear how many troops would be left in place beyond that time for policing, logistics, and consultative roles. Despite his pledge on Iraq and the resulting savings that will accrue from that decision, Obama promised to send more troops to Afghanistan and boost the elusively renamed "overseas contingency operations," which would garner $75.5 billion in supplemental appropriations for 2009 and $130 billion in 2010 (according to his proposed budget in April 2009). Overall, Pentagon spending would rise to $534 billion in 2010, a 4 percent hike over 2009. In addition, Obama wanted to raise military pay, improve veterans' health care, and boost the size of the Army and the Marine Corps. Although he was dovish on Iraq, he was hawkish on bolstering the Pentagon's many global missions while improving defense procurement policies to save money.

Being the global *gendarme* costs money, though, and the government will continue to borrow to remain top cop in the world without increased revenues or gargantuan spending cuts. Priorities need to shift because trillions are being wasted. If more than half of the gross domestic product (about $13 trillion) is being pledged to save the shrinking financial sector, Obama will need to take a knife to all bloated programs in order to save his progressive agenda—including those in the Pentagon. It's a political imperative. In a time in which financial bailout pledges amounted to $42,000 for every person in the United States, some reckoning was in order.

Where to Cut and Tax

Here's where true political courage comes into play. For every program, there is a sponsor (or group of congressional patrons) and often a sole individual or corporate beneficiary. Huge defense programs benefit contractors. Agricultural subsidies largely feather the bottom lines of multinational corporations. In every case, there is tremendous lobbying power behind each appropriation. If oxen are to be gored, then many well-heeled interests will do the squealing. If Obama wants to adhere to the progressive credo of rooting out wasteful programs and protecting taxpayers, this is where he can start:

- ◆ **Repatriate corporate income.** Corporations have been "offshoring" income in shell corporations outside of the reach of the Internal Revenue Service for decades. According to the U.S. Government Accountability Office (GAO), 83 of the 100 largest publicly traded U.S. corporations had subsidiaries in countries known as tax havens; these account for about $1 trillion in past earnings, according to the GAO. That means that corporations enjoy all of the corporate benefits of doing business in the world's largest economy but without paying their full tax bills and depriving the country of needed revenue. This needs to be a top priority for the Obama administration in coming years, although it will be like rolling a boulder uphill to fight corporate lobbying. The administration has moved to obtain information on offshored money in Swiss bank accounts and had several other corporate income repatriation proposals.

- ◆ **Rework and reduce agricultural subsidies.** For years, agricultural subsidies have veered from their original goals of keeping families in farming and protecting farmers against acts of nature such as floods and drought. As the farm bill became an obese serving of checks to huge agricultural combines, the Depression-era protections became perversely skewed toward the undeserving. The ethanol subsidy alone (just for farmers) is $20 billion over five years through 2015; this money goes toward growing corn for a fuel that does little to reduce pollution, sucks up (and later taints) water supplies, and does almost nothing to reduce the amount of imported oil. All told, the taxpayer group Citizens Against Government Waste (CAGW) estimates that some $84 billion could be trimmed from farm spending. Obama's auditors could also overhaul nearly every commodity subsidy program, from milk to corn, to focus on value-added, healthy organic crops.

- ◆ **Cut bloated defense spending.** Though there are still real threats to the security of U.S. citizens, many programs fail to provide comprehensive security in the twenty-first century. Although Defense Secretary Gates proposed cutting orders for the F-22 fighter jet and $1.4 billion of the unproven missile defense program (as of mid-April 2009), he was just scratching the surface of potential savings, especially in light of the U.S. involvement in Afghanistan and Iraq. The United States could probably cancel the F-35 joint strike fighter program (for updated fighter planes) and instead upgrade F/A-18s, allowing the government to pocket $22 billion over five years. The government could also cancel the "Future Combat System" (a high-tech battle device) and save $11 billion. Just by eliminating payments for independent research (contractors who are probably overpaid), another $14 billion could be realized. All told, the CAGW estimates that Pentagon cuts could put a quarter of a trillion dollars back into the Treasury. This money could go toward a down payment on a universal health-care system. Do we still need troops in Europe and Japan? The CAGW's numbers are just a start in reconsidering our global military spending.

- ◆ **Reconsider inflation-adjusted costs.** Gasoline taxes have not changed since 1993. At the very least, these taxes should be adjusted for inflation (along with other excise taxes), which would bring in at least $5 billion into the Treasury over five years (ending in 2015). Climate-related events could cost Americans trillions, and it is no longer possible to expect the private insurance industry to cover this global calamity. Everything from wildfires in the West to floods in the Midwest and hurricanes on the East Coast will continue to ravage taxpayers. Inflation adjusting provides a new lens for the progressive agenda because the government's consumer price index rarely shows its true impact on average households; it's a bureaucratic fiction that helps employers keep salary increases down and Social Security benefit adjustments low. The purchasing power of the dollar dropped 18 percent during the Bush years. That means that you had to make up that amount in your paycheck just to stay even. Of course, that's just an average: excluding food and fuel (a neat sleight of hand the government consistently plays), college fees climbed 248 percent from 1990 through 2008, hospital services rose 222 percent, dental care rose 153 percent, and prescription drugs went up 120 percent.

◆ **Tackle employer and home subsidies.** These will be among the most painful and radical decisions to make, yet they will be necessary if the Obama camp is to go beyond rhetoric. Nearly every analyst agrees that one of the most basic principles of health reform is that every health consumer must know how *much* their benefit costs. Right now, this is not possible because more than 60 percent of the population has third-party coverage and because employers receive a $300 billion–plus annual tax break to provide the benefit. Cutting this subsidy is certainly not the only piece of the complex health-reform puzzle, but it is a necessary first step in unlinking health care from employment and creating a portable, affordable, and flexible package. Perhaps an even more sacred cow is the write-off for home mortgage interest, which is currently the largest subsidy given to taxpayers who itemize on their tax returns. Almost a half trillion dollars was diverted from the Treasury for this write-off in 2006 (the most recent available data), followed by a quarter trillion for state and local taxes. The fundamental question that needs to be asked is: Did these breaks artificially inflate housing prices and somehow facilitate the resulting crash? If so, should taxpayers still subsidize housing in this way? The real estate, building, and banking industries are monolithic opponents to touching this sacred cow, arguing that it would lead to a further collapse in housing prices. Maybe allowing the free market to determine home values—without the distortions of subsidies—would make housing more affordable for everyone. It's worthy of study.

◆ **Root out wasteful government contracting.** The U.S. Treasury routinely overpays billions of people on almost 4 million contracts, wasting about $100 billion annually. Many nonperforming contractors were paid *bonuses*—about $8 billion from 1999 to 2005—even on botched assignments. A thorough audit of contracting is imperative if Obamanomics is to be fully accountable to taxpayers.

◆ **Fix the tax code.** At more than 10,000 pages, the cornucopia of giveaways still favors well-heeled taxpayers who can hire firms to shield income or hide it from Uncle Sam. The IRS estimates that at least $300 billion is lost every year from those who avoid taxes. Restoring marginal rates to the pre-Bush era would pump another $500 billion to $600 billion back into government coffers and offer fewer breaks for the top 1 percent of the population. Simplicity would also mean transparency. With fewer ways of hiding money, the government could take in more revenue and finance such important social programs as universal health care. Obama talked about restoring "fairness and balance" to the tax code on April 15, although he didn't launch a specific initiative to reform tax laws at that time.

◆ **Improve energy efficiency and carbon neutrality.** Buildings consume as much as 40 percent of the nation's energy and are profligate wasters of resources. The Obama administration has already provided numerous tax incentives for greening every structure, from a single-family home to public housing, but more needs to be done. The administration needs to put in place a long-term program with the specific goals of energy and greenhouse gas reduction in order to achieve carbon neutrality within a generation. As with speculation penalties, resource and energy waste should be taxed to change behaviors. There is no reason why every building can't be green and why the United States can't build an export industry around green technologies. The world needs these ideas. Our survival mandates it.

Restraining Market Forces

Another measure of the success of the Obama agenda will be how well it serves as a guardian against metaphorical "black swans." In the harshest realities of market forces, these beasts have consumed more than $30 trillion worldwide over the past few years. Retirement fund balances have evaporated, forcing drastic changes in how most Americans plan for their golden years. Home equity, which was always regarded as the safest of nest eggs, is eroding by the day.

Under the tenets of the ownership society, we are all free to make our own choices in retirement funds, mortgages, credit cards, and any number of financial decisions. Unfortunately, no one who truly believes in this brave new world of unfettered market economics has bothered to reveal the men behind the curtains pulling all the levers. If the curtains were pulled back, we would see a lot of smoke and mirrors.

Most investors in 401(k)s have no idea what they are doing. Should they put all of their money in company stock? This was a bad idea for the people whose boardrooms and CEOs were concealing fraud, as was the case with Enron and WorldCom. Few people, if any, have any idea what shadows lurk on—or off—corporate balance sheets. Profits, debts, and side deals can be moved out of sight and, in many cases, out of the country. What about those safe mutual funds? Most employers never bother to tell their employees how much middlemen take in fees. In many cases, workers are being gouged for their own retirement plans, sometimes paying four layers of hidden fees in addition to paying for poor fund management. And then those who thought they would always have value in their homes had to let go of that myth in early 2007 with the fall of the housing market, necessitating the emergence of Obama and his ongoing rescue plan.

Debunking the myths of the ownership society became a priority in the Obama campaign, although millions of people had seen a myriad of market-driven losses long before Obama arrived on the national scene. Less than ten years ago, in the late 1990s, venture capitalists backed any project followed by "dot-com"; these projects were then sold by Wall Street brokers and hawked to the unwashed masses salivating over an early retirement. When that bubble burst, resulting in the 2001 recession, the former Federal Reserve chief Alan Greenspan lowered interest rates as President Bush and Congress lowered taxes. With easy money, millions of people believed the market was finally on their side and responded by buying property. Not only could they make money on their homes, they thought, but also they could make money on *any* property and flip it for a profit to some lesser fool.

If anything, the sting of the ownership society deception was that people need protection *from* the market. Big institutions have protection in the form of insurance and portfolio hedging. If the government runs into trouble financing its countless giveaways, it can

Obamanomics and Market Regulation: A Blueprint

This is a broad outline of how the Obama team plans to tackle financial market regulation or, in his words, the reality that "strong financial markets require clear rules of the road."

- Concentrate on systemic risk and enforce strict oversight on institutions that can cause the most damage to the global financial system.
- Strengthen markets so that they can withstand the failure of one large institution and systemwide stress.
- Mandate transparency and "speak in plain language investors can understand."
- Supervise financial products based on "actual data on how people make financial decisions."
- Hold market players accountable, particularly executives.
- Overhaul regulations so that they are comprehensive.
- Recognize global challenges. A regulator of markets across borders is needed.

print more money. But what can average homeowners making $50,000 a year do? No longer are their pensions guaranteed. In most cases, no longer are there unions to back them up if companies renege on benefits (more than 80 percent of the workforce is nonunionized). At the height of the housing bubble, even Greenspan was encouraging homeowners to obtain adjustable-rate mortgages, exposing people to bond-market and repayment risk.

It will take years for Obama's team to reestablish the New Deal protections that were carved up and thrown away over the past thirty years. Where would they start? Here are a few considerations they are working on:

- ♦ **Financial regulation overhaul.** The New Deal protections worked when there were only banks and brokers in the financial sphere. Now banks, brokers, nonbanks, insurance companies, pension funds, government funds, and hedge funds are all connected through an utterly bewildering web of derivatives, bonds, stocks, and securities that few laypeople understand. A super-regulator, perhaps working with or through the Federal Reserve banks, needs to be a good cop over "systemic" risk, the kind of debacles that can happen when everyone is connected to the same global financial network. Led by Obama adviser Paul Volcker, an organization called the Group of Thirty published a template for global oversight. It's international in scope and will require every regulator of a large industrial economy to sign onto and enforce. Without such a framework, more global meltdowns are guaranteed. A global super-regulator might emerge from this proposal, or a separate agency that looks out specifically for the rights of individual investors. Since regulators such as the Securities and Exchange Commission, Financial Industry Regulatory Authority, Federal Reserve, and Commodity Futures Trading Commission failed investors during the market meltdown of 2008, some kind of consolidation or separation of the agencies begs some serious action.

- ♦ **Redefining and restructuring the retirement safety net.** It is ludicrous to assume that 401(k)-type plans should remain as mainstream pension plans, which they were never designed to be. Guaranteed, annuitized programs that don't subject participants to market risk are essential in the progressive social contract. It will be a difficult transition as workers, employers, and government will all have to contribute—and sacrifice— something. Economist Teresa Ghilarducci at the New School for Social Research proposes a guaranteed retirement plan that would replace the 401(k) with an account that has a stable 3 percent rate of return above inflation. European countries all have something like this, but nothing will change without a partnership between the private and public sectors. *Social Security may even be expanded* to provide a higher percentage of pre-retirement income. That may mean higher payroll taxes, though.

♦ **Sharing wealth or limiting speculation.** In a free society, it's the cost of doing business. People will gamble and speculate. Yet why not encourage long-term investing by imposing a tax on assets sold or transferred within two years or a similar levy on stock or real estate sales? Dean Baker, codirector of the Center for Economic and Policy Research, says such a tax could curb the worst excesses of the casino economy and raise about $100 billion to $150 billion per year (with a 0.25 percent fee) on stock transactions. We can have compassionate capitalism, but it has to have some circuit breakers to discourage short-term speculation; executive, broker, and money management greed; and sheer recklessness in financial engineering.

♦ **Encouraging sustainability.** Ultimately, this is the mother of all guiding principles. Bank lending and real estate prices were unsustainable. Retirement plans that invested in stocks blew up. People who had adjustable-rate loans that reset to higher rates lost their homes. Suburban sprawl fed the housing debacle and fouled the air and water. We are pumping far too much carbon dioxide into the atmosphere and devouring more resources than our fragile planet can handle. We have yet to build a twenty-first-century economic and educational system to address these and many other crises. It would be a triumph of Obamanomics if his tenure managed to effectively address even one of these issues. The administration can offer tax rebates for inner-city development and pedestrian-friendly neighborhoods. It can redirect subsidies from military expenditures to provide at-home care not only for the elderly but also for children and the disabled. If the Obama administration is serious, then it can rewrite a stronger social contract, reform tax policy (and the 10,000-page tax code nightmare), and ensure a decent future for many generations to come. Political leverage can be applied judiciously to achieve a host of progressive goals.

Who Will Pay?

As I write this, the national debt is $11 trillion and climbing. The difference between the federal government's revenue and payments—the budget deficit—is $1 trillion plus *and climbing*. Economists and policy makers see no other choice but to buoy the financial system with borrowed money, but there is a nagging question for future generations: How will all this money be paid back? Will hyperinflation ravage the economy further when the government needs to pay investors higher rates of return on its debt?

None of this fiscal manic depression is sustainable. Certainly some huge sacrifices will be made in terms of government program cutbacks or higher taxes. The outstanding liability for all social programs, debt repayment, and other government services is about $34 trillion, reports the Peterson Foundation. That's more than twice the size of our current economy.

The Obamanomics mission will need to reframe whole arguments to move the American political class away from the fallacies of market economics and supply-side mythology. FDR instilled the idea of "Freedom from Want." Why not guarantee medical care and retirement benefits through a constitutional amendment? Some people might say this national call to arms is outrageous, but it's nothing less than a human right, one that transcends politics.

Ultimately, Obama and his allies will be judged on how well they restore and maintain prosperity—that is, how they will remake or simply *preserve* the American Dream. As he said in his inaugural address, "the success of our economy has always depended not just on the size of our gross national product, but on the reach of our prosperity; on our ability to extend opportunity to every willing heart—not out of charity, but because it is the surest route to our common good."

Appendix

This appendix presents a detailed list of spending in the Recovery Act or stimulus plan (totals for each category are in bold at the top of each table column).

Accountability	$323,500,000
Department of Agriculture: Office of Inspector General (OIG)	$22,500,000
Department of Commerce: OIG	$10,000,000
National Oceanic and Atmospheric Administration (NOAA): OIG	$6,000,000
Department of Justice: OIG	$2,000,000
National Aeronautics and Space Administration (NASA): OIG	$2,000,000
Defense Department: OIG	$15,000,000
Department of Energy: OIG	$15,000,000
Department of the Treasury: Inspector General for Tax Administration	$7,000,000
General Services Administration: OIG	$7,000,000
Recovery Act Accountability and Transparency Board	$84,000,000
Small Business Administration: OIG	$10,000,000
Department of Homeland Security: OIG	$5,000,000
Bureau of Indian Affairs: OIG	$15,000,000
Environmental Protection Agency: OIG	$20,000,000
Department of Labor: OIG	$6,000,000
Department of Health and Human Services (DHHS): OIG	$17,000,000

Continued

Source: All tables adapted from information at http://www.propublica.org/special/the-stimulus-plan-a-detailed-list-of-spending.

Accountability	$323,500,000
Department of Education: OIG	$14,000,000
Corporation for National and Community Service: OIG	$1,000,000
Social Security Administration: OIG	$2,000,000
Government Accountability Office: salaries and expenses	$25,000,000
Veterans Affairs: OIG	$1,000,000
State Department: OIG	$2,000,000
Department of Transportation: OIG	$20,000,000
Department of Housing and Urban Development: OIG	$15,000,000

Aid to People Affected by Economic Downturn	$36,910,807,000
Rural Housing Service insurance fund program account: direct loans and unsubsidized guaranteed loans	$11,672,000,000
Rural community facilities program account	$130,000,000
Special supplemental nutrition program for women, infants, and children	$500,000,000
School lunch programs for schools in which at least 50% of students are eligible for free or reduced-price meals	$100,000,000
Food-bank commodity assistance program	$150,000,000
Temporary increase in benefits under the Supplemental Nutrition Assistance Program (food stamps)	$19,900,000,000
Food-distribution program on Indian reservations	$5,000,000
Agricultural disaster assistance transition: Federal Crop Insurance Act farm operating loans	$173,367,000
Direct farm operating loans	$20,440,000
IRS health insurance tax-credit administration	$80,000,000
Emergency food and shelter	$100,000,000
Bureau of Indian Affairs job-training and housing-improvement programs	$40,000,000
Indian guaranteed-loan program	$10,000,000
Community service employment for older Americans	$120,000,000
Extra funding for state unemployment insurance	$150,000,000
State reemployment services for the jobless	$250,000,000
Child care assistance for low-income families	$1,651,227,000
Child care assistance for low-income families through state programs	$255,186,000
Child care assistance for low-income families to improve infant and toddler care	$93,587,000
Community Service Block Grant Program	$1,000,000,000
Social Security Act funding	$50,000,000
Social Security Administration processing of disability and retirement workloads	$460,000,000

Aid to State and Local Governments	$58,355,000,000
State administration expenses to carry out increase in food stamp program	$295,000,000
Economic development assistance programs	$150,000,000
Violence against women prevention and prosecution programs	$225,000,000
Office of Justice Programs: state and local law-enforcement assistance (Edward Byrne Memorial Justice Assistance Grants)	$2,000,000,000
State and local law-enforcement assistance grants to improve criminal justice systems, assist crime victims, and mentor youth	$225,000,000
Southern border and high-intensity drug-trafficking areas	$30,000,000
ATF Project Gunrunner	$10,000,000
State and local law-enforcement assistance to Indian tribes	$225,000,000
Crime victim assistance	$100,000,000
Rural drug-crime program	$125,000,000
Internet crimes against children initiatives	$50,000,000
Community Oriented Policing Services (COPS) grants	$1,000,000,000
Justice Department salaries and expenses for administration of police grant programs	$10,000,000
Community Development Financial Institutions Fund for financial assistance, training, and outreach to Native American, Hawaiian, and Alaskan native communities	$100,000,000
Local and state fire-station upgrades and construction	$210,000,000
Disaster-assistance direct loans may exceed $5,000,000 and may be equal to not more than 50% of local government annual budget if the government lost 25% or more in tax revenues	
State Fiscal Stabilization Fund to avoid cutbacks and layoffs: 82% must be used for education while 18% may be used for public safety and other government services. The latter part may be used for repairs and modernization of K–12 schools and college and university buildings.	$53,600,000,000

Business	$870,000,000
Rural Business-Cooperative Service: rural-business program account	$150,000,000
Small Business Administration salaries and expenses, microloan program, and improvements to technology systems	$69,000,000
Surety bond guarantees' revolving fund	$15,000,000
Small-business loans	$636,000,000

Education	$48,420,000,000
State grants for adult job training	$500,000,000
State grants for youth job training and summer-employment opportunities	$1,200,000,000
Dislocated-worker job training	$1,250,000,000
YouthBuild USA program for high-school dropouts who reenroll in other schools	$50,000,000
Job training in emerging industries	$250,000,000
Job training in the renewable-energy field	$500,000,000
Head Start programs	$1,000,000,000
Early Head Start program expansion	$1,100,000,000
Education for the disadvantaged: elementary and secondary education	$10,000,000,000
Education for the disadvantaged: school-improvement grants	$3,000,000,000
Education impact aid	$100,000,000
School-improvement programs	$650,000,000
Innovation and improvement of elementary and secondary schools	$200,000,000
Special education funding under the Individuals with Disabilities Education Act	$12,200,000,000
Pell Grants for higher education	$15,840,000,000
Institute of Education data systems	$245,000,000
Institute of Education state data coordinators	$5,000,000
Dislocated-worker assistance national reserve	$200,000,000
School-improvement grants awarded based on the number of homeless students identified in a state	$70,000,000
Student-aid administrative costs	$60,000,000

Energy	$41,400,000,000
Energy-efficiency and conservation block grants	$3,200,000,000
Weatherization Assistance Program (increases maximum income level and maximum assistance)	$5,000,000,000
State energy program	$3,100,000,000
Advanced batteries manufacturing, including lithium-ion batteries, hybrid electrical systems, component manufacturers, and software designers	$2,000,000,000
Modernize electricity grid	$4,400,000,000
Electricity-grid worker training	$100,000,000
Fossil energy research and development	$3,400,000,000

Energy	$41,400,000,000
Uranium Enrichment Decontamination and Decommissioning Fund	$390,000,000
Department of Energy science programs	$1,600,000,000
Advanced Research Projects Agency	$400,000,000
Innovative-technology loan-guarantee program	$6,000,000,000
Western Area Power Administration construction and maintenance	$10,000,000
Bonneville Power Administration borrowing authority	$3,250,000,000
Western Area Power Administration borrowing authority	$3,250,000,000
Leading-edge biofuel projects	$500,000,000
Federal building conversion to high-performance green buildings	$4,500,000,000
Energy-efficiency federal vehicle-fleet procurement	$300,000,000

Health Care	$18,830,000,000
Indian Health Service information-technology and telehealth services	$85,000,000
Indian health facilities	$415,000,000
Grants for public-health centers	$500,000,000
Construction, renovation, equipment, and information technology for health centers	$1,500,000,000
National Health Service Corps funding	$75,000,000
Addressing health professions workforce shortage	$425,000,000
National Institutes of Health (NIH) grants and contracts to renovate nonfederal research facilities	$1,000,000,000
NIH grants and contracts for shared resources and equipment for grantees	$300,000,000
NIH fund to support scientific research	$7,400,000,000
NIH Common Fund	$800,000,000
NIH renovations of high-priority buildings at the Bethesda, Maryland, campus and at other locations	$500,000,000
Comparative effectiveness research	$300,000,000
Comparative effectiveness research by the NIH	$400,000,000
Comparative effectiveness research by the DHHS	$400,000,000
Office of the National Coordinator for Health Information Technology	$1,680,000,000
National Coordinator for Health Information Technology's regional or subnational efforts	$300,000,000

Continued

Health Care	$18,830,000,000
Department of Commerce health-care information enterprise-integration activities related to the Office of the National Coordinator for Health Information Technology	$20,000,000
DHHS computer and information-technology security	$50,000,000
DHHS Prevention and Wellness Fund	$1,000,000,000
Prevention and Wellness Fund immunization program	$300,000,000
Prevention and Wellness Fund evidence-based clinical and community-based prevention strategies	$650,000,000
Prevention and Wellness Fund reduction in incidence of health-care–associated infections	$50,000,000
Rehabilitation services and disability research	$540,000,000
State grants for rehabilitation services and disability research	$18,200,000
Rehabilitation services in independent-living centers	$87,500,000
Rehabilitation services for older blind individuals	$34,300,000

Other	$2,147,000,000
Census Bureau programs	$1,000,000,000
Digital-to-analog television converter-box program	$650,000,000
National Endowment for the Arts grants	$50,000,000
Department of Labor salaries and expenses	$80,000,000
Additional awards to existing AmeriCorps grantees	$83,000,000
AmeriCorps program salaries and expenses	$5,200,000
AmeriCorps program administrative costs of expansion	$800,000
National-security trust appropriation	$40,000,000
Social Security Administration health-information technology research	$40,000,000
Filipino World War II veterans compensation	$198,000,000

Science and Technology	$13,142,000,000
Farm Service Agency salaries and expenses to maintain and modernize the information-technology system	$50,000,000
Distance-learning, telemedicine, and broadband program	$2,500,000,000
National Telecommunications and Information Administration: broadband-technology opportunities program	$4,690,000,000
National Institute of Standards and Technology scientific and technical research and services	$220,000,000

Science and Technology	$13,142,000,000
NIST construction of research facilities	$360,000,000
NOAA operations, research, and facilities	$230,000,000
NOAA procurement, acquisition, and construction	$600,000,000
NASA science	$400,000,000
NASA aeronautics	$150,000,000
NASA exploration	$400,000,000
NASA cross-agency support	$50,000,000
National Science Foundation (NSF) research and related activities	$2,500,000,000
NSF education and human resources	$100,000,000
NSF major research equipment and facilities construction	$400,000,000
NSF OIG	$2,000,000
Veterans Affairs for hiring and training of claims processors	$150,000,000
Veterans Affairs information-technology systems	$50,000,000
State Department technology-security upgrades	$252,000,000
U.S. Agency for International Development (USAID) technology	$38,000,000

Transportation and Infrastructure	$98,325,000,000
Agriculture buildings and facilities and rental payments	$24,000,000
Agricultural Research Service buildings and facilities	$176,000,000
Natural Resources Conservation Service watershed and flood prevention	$290,000,000
Watershed-rehabilitation program	$50,000,000
Rural Utilities Service water and waste-disposal program account	$1,380,000,000
Department of Defense (DoD) facilities operation and maintenance, Army	$1,474,525,000
DoD facilities operation and maintenance, Navy	$657,051,000
DoD facilities operation and maintenance, Marine Corps	$113,865,000
DoD facilities operation and maintenance, Air Force	$1,095,959,000
DoD facilities operation and maintenance, Army Reserve	$98,269,000
DoD facilities operation and maintenance, Navy Reserve	$55,083,000
DoD facilities operation and maintenance, Marine Corps Reserve	$39,909,000
DoD facilities operation and maintenance, Air Force Reserve	$13,187,000

Continued

Transportation and Infrastructure	$98,325,000,000
DoD facilities operation and maintenance, Army National Guard	$266,304,000
DoD facilities operation and maintenance, Air National Guard	$25,848,000
Army research development, test and evaluation	$75,000,000
Navy research development, test and evaluation	$75,000,000
Air Force research development, test and evaluation	$75,000,000
Defense-wide research development, test and evaluation	$75,000,000
DoD medical facilities repair and modernization, including energy efficiency	$400,000,000
Corps of Engineers investigations	$25,000,000
Corps of Engineers construction	$2,000,000,000
Corps of Engineers: Mississippi River and tributaries	$375,000,000
Corps of Engineers operations and maintenance	$2,075,000,000
Corps of Engineers regulatory program	$25,000,000
Corps of Engineers formerly utilized sites remedial-action program	$100,000,000
Bureau of Reclamation water and related resources, including inspection of canals in urbanized areas	$900,000,000
Central Utah Project water programs	$50,000,000
California Bay–Delta restoration	$50,000,000
Nondefense environmental cleanup	$483,000,000
Defense environmental cleanup	$5,127,000,000
Federal buildings and courthouses	$750,000,000
Border stations and land ports of entry	$300,000,000
Department of Homeland Security headquarters consolidation	$200,000,000
Customs and Border Protection nonintrusive inspection systems	$100,000,000
Customs and Border Protection tactical communications equipment and radios	$60,000,000
Border security fencing, infrastructure, and technology	$100,000,000
Land border ports-of-entry construction	$420,000,000
Immigration and Customs Enforcement tactical-communications equipment and radios	$20,000,000
Transportation Security Administration checked-baggage and checkpoint explosives-detection machines	$1,000,000,000
Coast Guard shore facilities and aids to navigation facilities	$98,000,000
Coast Guard alteration of bridges	$142,000,000
FEMA public-transportation and railroad security	$150,000,000

Transportation and Infrastructure	$98,325,000,000
FEMA port-security grants	$150,000,000
Bureau of Land Management maintenance and restoration of facilities, trails, lands, abandoned mines, and wells	$125,000,000
Bureau of Land Management construction of roads, bridges, trails, and facilities, including energy-efficient retrofits	$180,000,000
Wildland fire management and hazardous-fuels reduction	$15,000,000
U.S. Fish and Wildlife Service maintenance and construction on wildlife refuges and fish hatcheries and for habitat restoration	$165,000,000
U.S. Fish and Wildlife Service roads, bridges, and facilities, including energy-efficient retrofits	$115,000,000
National Park Service facilities and trails	$146,000,000
Historically black colleges and universities preservation	$15,000,000
National Park Service road construction, cleanup of abandoned mines on parkland and other infrastructure	$589,000,000
U.S. Geological Survey facilities and equipment, including stream gauges, seismic and volcano-monitoring systems, and national map activities	$140,000,000
Bureau of Indian Affairs construction of roads, schools, and detention centers	$450,000,000
Superfund-site cleanup	$600,000,000
Leaking underground-storage-tank cleanup	$200,000,000
Clean-water state revolving-fund grants	$4,000,000,000
Safe-drinking-water capitalization grants	$2,000,000,000
Brownfields projects	$100,000,000
Diesel-emission–reduction grants and loans	$300,000,000
Forest Service road, bridge, and trail maintenance; watershed restoration; facilities improvement; remediation of abandoned mines; and support costs	$650,000,000
Wildfire mitigation	$500,000,000
Smithsonian Institution repairs	$25,000,000
Construction, renovation, and acquisition of Job Corps Centers	$250,000,000
Social Security Administration's National Computer Center replacement	$500,000,000
Military construction, Army: child-development centers and warrior-transition complexes	$180,000,000

Continued

Transportation and Infrastructure	$98,325,000,000
Military construction, Navy and Marine Corps: child-development centers and warrior-transition complexes	$280,000,000
Military construction, Air Force: child-development centers and warrior-transition complexes	$180,000,000
Military hospital-construction and energy-conservation investments	$1,450,000,000
Military construction, Army National Guard	$50,000,000
Military construction, Air National Guard	$50,000,000
Family-housing construction, Army	$34,507,000
Family-housing operation and maintenance, Army	$3,932,000
Family-housing construction, Air Force	$80,100,000
Family-housing operation and maintenance, Air Force	$16,461,000
Temporary expansion of military homeowner-assistance program to respond to mortgage foreclosure and credit crisis, including acquisition of property at or near military bases that have been ordered closed	$555,000,000
Veterans Affairs hospital maintenance	$1,000,000,000
National Cemetery Administration for monument and memorial repairs	$50,000,000
State extended-care facilities, such as nursing homes	$150,000,000
State Department diplomatic and consular programs for domestic passport and training facilities	$90,000,000
International Boundary and Water Commission: Rio Grande levee repairs	$220,000,000
Additional capital investments in surface transportation, including highways, bridges, and road repairs	$1,298,500,000
Administrative costs for additional capital investment in surface transportation	$200,000,000
Capital investments in surface transportation grants to be awarded by other administration	$1,500,000
Federal Aviation Administration infrastructure	$200,000,000
Grants-in-aid for airports	$1,100,000,000
Highway-infrastructure investment	$26,725,000,000
Highway-infrastructure investment in Puerto Rico	$105,000,000
Highway-infrastructure funds distributed by states	$60,000,000
Highway-infrastructure funds for the Indian Reservation Roads program	$550,000,000
Highway-infrastructure funds for surface-transportation technical training	$20,000,000
Highway infrastructure to fund oversight and management of projects	$40,000,000

Transportation and Infrastructure	$98,325,000,000
High-speed-rail capital assistance	$8,000,000,000
National Railroad passenger corporation (AMTRAK) capital grants	$850,000,000
National Railroad passenger corporation capital grants for security	$450,000,000
Federal Transit Administration capital assistance	$6,800,000,000
Public-transportation discretionary grants	$100,000,000
Fixed-guideway infrastructure investment	$750,000,000
Capital-investment grants	$750,000,000
Shipyard grants	$100,000,000
Public-housing capital improvements	$3,000,000,000
Public-housing renovations and energy-conservation investments	$1,000,000,000
Native American housing block grants	$510,000,000
Community-development funding	$1,000,000,000
Emergency assistance for the redevelopment of abandoned and foreclosed homes	$2,000,000,000
Additional capital investments in low-income housing tax-credit projects	$2,250,000,000
Homelessness prevention and rehousing	$1,500,000,000
Assistance to owners of properties receiving Section 8 assistance	$2,000,000,000
Grants and loans for green investment in Section 8 properties	$250,000,000
Lead-hazard reduction	$100,000,000

Resources

Note: This is a condensed bibliographic essay. The citations are for each chapter, but they are not assigned to specific pages.

INTRODUCTION

Throughout the book, I refer to Obama's political manifesto, *The Audacity of Hope* (Crown, 2006), and his superlative autobiography, *Dreams from My Father: A Story of Race and Inheritance* (Three Rivers Press, 2004).

All references to economic conditions were from Bloomberg News from 2008 through April 17, 2009 (and my own columns for that news service), except for "Foreclosures Soar 81 Percent in 2008" by Lynn Adler, Reuters, Jan. 15, 2009; and "Stock Losses Leave Pensions Underfunded by $400 Billion," by David Hilzenrath, *Washington Post*, Jan. 7, 2009.

For background on the Depression, I referred to T. H. Watkins's classic *The Great Depression: America in the 1930s* (Blackside, 1993), and Amity Shlaes's "A Chilling Uncertainty: The Lessons of Roosevelt's Experimentation," *Washington Post*, Dec. 31, 2008. I also referred to her *The Forgotten Man: A New History of the Great Depression* (Harper Perennial, 2008).

The majority of the pledges from the Obama–Biden campaign throughout the book were taken (in most cases, word for word)

from the Obama–Biden Web sites: www.mybarackobama.com, www
.barackobama.com, and www.change.gov, a transitional site.

I was "on the ground" in Chicago on election day, 2008.

CHAPTER 1

The chronological background for the economic crisis was taken from
Bloomberg News stories.

All references to the "stimulus plan" or "stimulus package" are from the
American Recovery and Reinvestment Act of 2009. Most of the material
is from the House Ways and Means Committee summaries at http://
waysandmeans.house.gov/MoreInfo.asp?section=50 or from the White
House site: www.whitehouse.gov. The paper titled *Job Impact of the American Recovery and Reinvestment Plan* by administration economists Jared
Bernstein and Christina Romer from Jan. 9, 2009, also was helpful.

I also referred to stimulus plan summaries from the Associated
Press, U.S. Department of Education, and ProPublica's "The Stimulus
Plan: A Detailed List of Spending" (www.propublica.org).

All references to the "2010 budget document" are from the
Obama administration's budget proposal, which is entitled "A New
Era of Responsibility: Renewing America's Promise," from the Office
of Management and Budget: www.budget.gov. It's more of a series of
outlines, summaries, and essays such as "Jumpstarting the Economy
and Investing for the Future." Because it doesn't contain any "hard" numbers on specific programs, it's a detailed guideline for Congress, which
makes the final decisions on the administration's proposals through its
appropriations process, which was continuing as this went to press.

I referenced to "Fixing Finance," from *The Economist*, Jan. 22,
2009; the U.S. Internal Revenue Service Web site (www.irs.gov);
"COBRA Premiums for Family Health Coverage Consume 84 Per-
cent of Unemployment Benefits," press release and study from
Families USA, Jan. 9, 2009 (www.familiesusa.org); Robert Kuttner's
*Obama's Challenge: America's Economic Crisis and the Power of a
Transformative President* (Chelsea Green, 2008); Jonathan Alter's
*The Defining Moment: FDR's Hundred Days and the Triumph of
Hope* (Simon & Schuster, 2007); "An $800 Billion Mistake" by
Martin Feldstein, *Washington Post*, Jan. 29, 2009; "The Bottom

Line on Obamanomics," by David Leonhardt, *International Herald Tribune* (also appeared in the *New York Times Magazine*), Aug. 22, 2008; and "Mythbusting the Obama Recovery Package," by Sara Robinson, Campaign for America's Future (www.ourfuture.org), Jan. 8, 2009.

CHAPTER 2

I relied on the *Washington Post's* summary, "2010 Budget Blueprint: Agency by Agency" (www.washingtonpost.com), as well as the Office of Management and Budget's summaries.

I also referred to "Big Ideas, Grand Plans, Modest Budgets" by Michael Cooper, *New York Times*, Feb. 15, 2009; daily coverage at www.politico.com; "The Report Card on America's Infrastructure" by the American Society of Civil Engineers (www.asce.org) from Jan. 29, 2009; "'Ready to Go' Jobs and Infrastructure Projects: America's Mayors Report to the Nation on Projects to Strengthen Metro Economies and Create Jobs Now" by the U.S. Conference of Mayors (www.usmayors.org); "Stimulus Bill Sends Thrill through Region," by Daniel de Vise and John Wagner, *Washington Post*, Jan. 27, 2009; "Compiling a To-Do List for Obama's New Deal," by Jonathan Weisman, *Wall Street Journal*, Dec. 18, 2008; "Good Building, Bad Building," by Eric Lotke, www.ourfuture.org blog, Dec. 10, 2008; "Issues and Options in Infrastructure Investment" by the Congressional Budget Office, May 2008 (www.cbo.gov); "ETFs for Infrastructure," by John Spence, Jan. 5, 2009, www.marketwatch.com; *iMoney: Profitable Exchange-Traded Fund Strategies for Every Investor*, by Thomas Lydon and John F. Wasik (FT Press, 2008); and "Qwest, Danaher May Gain from Obama Spending Plan," by Thomas Black, Bloomberg News, Dec. 30, 2008.

CHAPTER 3

For insight and criticism of Obama's small-business policies, I referenced "Small Businesses Critical of Stimulus," by Mickey Meece, *New York Times*, Feb. 7, 2009; "Small-Business Agency

Prodded to Spur Lending," by Brady Dennis, *Washington Post*, April 9, 2009; *The Small Business Economy: A Report to the President*, by the U.S. Small Business Administration, 2008; the Office of Management and Budget's "New Era of Responsibility" (see above); the Kauffman Foundation's "2008 State New Economy Index," Nov. 18, 2008, and telephone interview with the foundation's Robert Litan on Jan. 30, 2009; "A Lifeline for Small Business," by Maura Reynolds, *Chicago Tribune*, March 17, 2009; "American Recovery and Reinvestment Act of 2009: Cost Estimate," by the Congressional Budget Office (www.cbo.gov), Feb. 2, 2009; "Senate Leaders Reach $780 Billion Compromise," by Greg Hitt and Jonathan Weisman, Feb. 7–8, 2009, *Wall Street Journal*; "The New Squeeze: How a Perfect Storm of Bad Mortgages and Credit Card Debt Could Paralyze the Economy," by Jose Garcia, Demos (www.demos. org), Nov. 13, 2008; "Green Collar Jobs Report," American Solar Energy Society (www.ases.org), Jan. 26, 2009; "How Obama Can Boost the Economy by Investing in Science," by the editors of *Scientific American*, Jan. 20, 2009; "Clean Energy Is the Foundation of Proposed Stimulus," The Apollo Alliance (www.apolloalliance. org), Jan. 23, 2009; and "Factors Underlying the Decline in Manufacturing Employment Since 2000," by the Congressional Budget Office, Dec. 23, 2008.

CHAPTER 4

Most of the coverage of the Obama speeches was transcribed from live broadcasts on www.washingtonpost.com or www.cspan.org. I also referred to "Obama: 'Crisis' Worsening without Action," by Peter Nicholas, The Swamp (blog) on www.chicagotribune.com; "Too Little Bang for the Bucks," by Robert Samuelson, *Washington Post*, Feb. 2, 2009; "Small Is Profitable" (executive summary) from the Rocky Mountain Institute (www.smallisprofitable.org); "New Energy Finance Sees Year of Consolidation for Clean Energy in 2009," New Energy Finance press release, Jan. 23, 2009; "Recovery Plan Offers Needed Change," Center for American Progress (www.americanprogress.org), Jan. 16, 2009; "Career Center," www .greenbiz.com, Dec. 30, 2008; "Green Collar Jobs Are Poised for Growth," www.hotjobs.yahoo.com; and "The 2030 Challenge Stimulus Plan," www.architecture2030.org, Dec. 31, 2008.

CHAPTER 5

The bulk of the detailed breakdown of education programs is from the U.S. Department of Education's Web site and summaries at www .ed.gov and the 2010 budget document.

I also referred to "Stimulus Includes $5 Billion Flexible Fund for Education," by Maria Glod, *Washington Post*, Feb. 14, 2009; "Education Standards Likely to See Toughening," by Sam Dillon, *New York Times*, April 15, 2009, and the same reporter's "Stimulus Plan Would Provide Flood of Aid to Education," Jan. 28, 2009; "Student Debt and Defaults Surge," by Brendan Conway, *Christian Science Monitor*, April 7, 2009; "The Battle over Student Lending," editorial, *New York Times*, April 16, 2009; and background research and interviews with the Children's Leadership Council, Feb. 24, 2009.

Background on college costs and projected future income from graduates was from the College Board's "Trends in Higher Education 2008" (www.collegeboard.com/trends). Other material was obtained from www.finaid.com and IRS Publication 970, "Tax Benefits for Education" (www.irs.gov). The Project on Student Debt (www .projectonstudentdebt.org) also provided some figures.

CHAPTER 6

The background on the bank-recovery plan is from the U.S. Treasury (http://ustreas.gov) and the Federal Deposit Insurance Corporation (www.fdic.gov).

Credit-card and other lending abuses have been extensively documented by the Center for Responsible Lending (www .responsiblelending.org); see the center's report "Steered Wrong: Brokers, Borrowers and Subprime Loans," April 2008. The U.S. Government Accountability Office (www.gao.gov) has also documented credit-card fees in several reports. I also referred to Consumers Union's "Unfinished Business: Consumers Need More Protection from Unfair Credit Card Practices" (www.consumersunion.org),

Dec. 19, 2008. I also referred to "Prepayment Penalties Trap Many Borrowers," by John Hechinger, *Wall Street Journal*, April 10, 2009; and "Banking Regulators Finalize Credit Card Rules," *CFA News* (Consumer Federation of America), Oct.–Dec. 2008.

CHAPTER 7

Most of the housing-recovery plan was not part of the stimulus package and was included in the Treasury Department's Homeowner Affordability and Stability Plan. For a detailed summary, see www .treasury.gov/press/releases/tg33.htm.

I also referred to "The Growing Foreclosure Crisis," by Dina ElBoghdady and Sarah Cohen, *Washington Post*, Jan. 17, 2009; the 2010 budget document; and www.realtytrac.com.

CHAPTER 8

Many policy books examine the health-care crisis and propose solutions. Among the most influential are *Healthcare, Guaranteed* by Dr. Ezekiel Emanuel (Public Affairs, 2008); *The Healthcare Fix: Universal Insurance for All Americans*, by Laurence Kotlikoff (MIT Press, 2007); and Thomas Daschle's *Critical: What We Can Do About the Health-Care Crisis* (St. Martin's, 2008).

I also referred to "The Travails of Tom Daschle," editorial, *New York Times,* Feb. 3, 2009; "Ruin Your Health with the Obama Stimulus Plan," by Betsy McCaughey, Bloomberg News (commentary), Feb. 9, 2009; multiple reports from the Commonwealth Fund (www .commonwealthfund.org), most notably its "President's Message 2008/You Can Get There From Here: Mapping the Way to a Trans-formed US Health System," by Karen Davis; "In Hospital Deaths from Medical Errors at 195,000 per Year USA," *Medical News Today*, Aug. 9, 2004; "Update on Landmark Study on Single-Payer as Economic Stimulus," from California Nurses Association (www .calnurses.org), and multiple interviews and emails with Donna Smith, an organizer with the organization; multiple reports from the Kaiser Family Foundation (www.kff.org), particularly its "Annual Survey of Large and Small Employers" and survey "Growing Number of

Americans Report Problems Paying Medical Bills and Delaying and Skipping Care Due to Costs" (Oct. 21, 2008); "Obama's Health-Care Headache," by Robert Samuelson, *Washington Post*, Jan. 12, 2009; and "Accounting for the Cost of U.S. Health Care: A New Look at Why Americans Spend More," a McKinsey Global Institute Study, Dec. 2008.

One of Obama's first pronouncements on national health care was in his seminal speech before the Democratic National Convention in Boston, July 27, 2004.

CHAPTER 9

The annual trustees' report for Social Security, an extensive document of projections and assumptions, is at www.ssa.gov. The corresponding report on Medicare is at www.cms.hhs.gov/Reports TrustFunds/. Both reports are updated annually. I referred to the 2008 report of each agency. For more detailed analyses of the Social Security trust funds, I pored through the "Status of the Social Security and Medicare Programs," www.socialsecurity.gov/OACT/TRSUM/trsummary.html.

I also referred to "Obama Pledges Entitlement Reform," by Michael Shear, *Washington Post*, Jan. 16, 2009.

My main source on the long-term care section was Howard Gleckman's "How Can We Improve Long-Term Care Financing," from the Center for Retirement Research at Boston College (crr .bc.edu), June 2008. I also attended a retirement seminar at the college in Boston in October 2008 and referred to the center's report, "Are Retirement Savings Too Exposed to Market Risk," by Alicia Munnell and Dan Muldoon, Oct. 2008.

CHAPTER 10

There's a wealth of good writing on the "new" economy, humanistic economics, and redefining the global economic system. One of the foremost authorities is David Korten, whose book *Agenda for a New Economy: From Phantom Wealth to Real Wealth* (BK, 2009) is the most influential; Joel Magnuson's *Mindful Economics* (Seven Stories

Press, 2008); Riane Eisler's *The Real Wealth of Nations* (BK 2008); Thomas Friedman's *Hot, Flat, and Crowded: Why We Need a Green Revolution—and How It Can Renew America* (FSG, 2008); and Paul Krugman's *The Return of Depression Economics and the Crisis of 2008* (Norton, 2009). Also see www.p-ced.com for a primer of "people-centered economics."

I also referred to Obama's comments on the fiscal year 2010 budget from the White House blog (www.whitehouse.gov/the_press_office); Bloomberg News's estimate of $12.8 trillion in bank bailout pledges; "2009 Cost of Living Guide" by the American Institute for Economic Research (www.aier.org); "Budget Priorities," *Tikkun*, Nov.–Dec. 2008; "Bank Bailout Could Cost $4 Trillion," by Colin Barr, cnnmoney.com, Jan. 27, 2009; "International Taxation," GAO Report 09-157 (www.gao.gov), Dec. 2008; "Mr. Gates's Budget," editorial, *New York Times*, April 8, 2009; and "House, Senate Pass Budget Plans," Associated Press, April 3, 2009.

For an extensive list of wasteful government programs, refer to the "Prime Cuts 2009 Database," compiled by the Citizens Against Government Waste (www.cagw.org) and David Dietz's "Hidden Bonuses Enrich Government Contractors at Taxpayer Cost," Jan. 1, 2009.

A useful working document for global financial regulatory reform is "Financial Reform: A Framework for Financial Stability," by the Group of Thirty (www.group30.org/pubs/recommendations.pdf).

A seminal book on retirement-plan reform is Teresa Ghilarducci's *When I'm Sixty-Four: The Plot Against Pensions and the Plan to Save Them* (Princeton, 2008).

Index

About the Author

John F. Wasik is the award-winning author of twelve other books, including *The Cul-de-Sac Syndrome* and *The Merchant of Power*. He writes a biweekly column for Bloomberg News that reaches readers on five continents, and he also speaks widely. In addition, he is the cofounder and president of the not-for-profit Citizens Action Project (www.citizensactionproject.org), an activist group dedicated to fair, open, and accountable government. For more on his work, see www.johnwasik.com. For updates to the book and a related blog, see www.audacityofhelp.net.

About Bloomberg

BLOOMBERG L.P., founded in 1981, is a global information services, news, and media company. Headquartered in New York, Bloomberg has sales and news operations worldwide.

Serving customers on six continents, Bloomberg, through its wholly-owned subsidiary Bloomberg Finance L.P., holds a unique position within the financial services industry by providing an unparalleled range of features in a single package known as the Bloomberg Professional® service. By addressing the demand for investment performance and efficiency through an exceptional combination of information, analytic, electronic trading, and straight-through-processing tools, Bloomberg has built a worldwide customer base of corporations, issuers, financial intermediaries, and institutional investors.

Bloomberg News, founded in 1990, provides stories and columns on business, general news, politics, and sports to leading newspapers and magazines throughout the world. Bloomberg Television, a 24-hour business and financial news network, is produced and distributed globally in seven languages. Bloomberg Radio is an international radio network anchored by flagship station Bloomberg 1130 (WBBR-AM) in New York.

In addition to the Bloomberg Press line of books, Bloomberg publishes *Bloomberg Markets* magazine.

To learn more about Bloomberg, call a sales representative at:

London:	+44-20-7330-7500
New York:	+1-212-318-2000
Tokyo:	+81-3-3201-8900